Database Design and Modeling with Google Cloud

Learn database design and development to take your data to applications, analytics, and AI

Abirami Sukumaran

BIRMINGHAM—MUMBAI

Database Design and Modeling with Google Cloud

Group Product Manager: Reshma Raman
Publishing Product Manager: Heramb Bhavsar
Book Project Manager: Kirti Pisat
Content Development Editor: Manikandan Kurup, Joseph Sunil
Technical Editor: Rahul Limbachiya
Copy Editor: Safis Editing
Proofreader: Safis Editing
Indexer: Subalakshmi Govindhan
Production Designer: Jyoti Kadam
Senior DevRel Marketing Coordinator: Nivedita Singh

First published: December 2023

Production reference: 1121223

Published by Packt Publishing Ltd.
Grosvenor House
11 St Paul's Square
Birmingham
B3 1RB, UK.

ISBN 978-1-80461-145-6

www.packtpub.com

To my mother, Janaki, for her unconditional love

To the memory of my father, Sukumaran, for inspiring me to be who I am

To the memory of my grandparents Lakshmi, Srinivasan, and family to whom I owe everything

To my beloved country and friends for nurturing my soul

And to God for giving me resilience

Forewords

Databases are essential to the modern enterprise, as we all know. They store and manage our data, which is the lifeblood of our businesses. However, designing and modeling a database is not straightforward. It requires a deep understanding of the business, technology, and data.

Database Design and Modeling with Google Cloud, by Abirami Sukumaran, provides a comprehensive and practical guide to cloud database design and modeling. It serves as a compass for data professionals aiming to design and model databases that not only meet but exceed the demands of the modern, fast-paced digital era.

Abirami is a seasoned database practitioner and leader with almost two decades of experience in the databases and analytics field. She has worked with a wide range of businesses, from startups to large enterprises, and has helped them design and implement successful database applications. In this book, Abirami shares her wealth of experience by providing an organized approach to database design, and she shows you how to use Google Cloud to build scalable, reliable, and secure database applications.

One of the book's strengths lies in its inclusivity and relevance, addressing structured, semi-structured, and unstructured data considerations. The practical insights coupled with examples showcase the versatility of Google Cloud services in handling diverse data types, empowering readers to make informed decisions in their database design journey.

The hands-on approach is evident as the book leverages Google Cloud services, such as Cloud SQL, Spanner, BigQuery, Firestore, and Cloud Storage, to illustrate concepts in real-world applications. It goes beyond the traditional boundaries of database design, extending into the integration of databases with artificial intelligence through Vertex AI APIs and generative AI examples. This forward-thinking approach positions you to smoothly transition from data management to leveraging AI in their applications.

Whether you are a database novice or a seasoned professional, this book will help you take your database skills to the next level. I highly recommend this book to anyone who wants to learn more about cloud database design and modeling. It is a valuable resource that will help you design your databases thoughtfully and improve the performance of your applications centered around data.

Priyanka Vergadia

Head of North America Cloud Developer Advocacy

Google

It is an honor to write the foreword for this book, *Database Design and Modeling with Google Cloud*, by Abirami Sukumaran. She has poured her heart and soul into this work, a testament to her passion and dedication to empowering developers through technology.

In the age of AI and cloud, data is the new currency. A well-designed and futuristically modeled database can provide a solid foundation for speed, agility, efficiency, and scalability. However, navigating this rapidly evolving data and technology landscape can be complicated and daunting. Abirami Sukumaran's book emerges as a lighthouse, guiding practitioners through a holistic and pragmatic approach to designing databases that meet the demands of the digital age and empower organizations to thrive in a data-centric environment.

This book is a journey of discovery, learning, and growth. The journey commences with a strategic exploration of business and technical considerations that set the stage for effective database design. It equips you with the ability to ask the right questions, make informed decisions, and navigate the endless possibilities of cloud-based databases. It leads you through an immersive, hands-on experience, navigating the complexities of different data formats and real-world use cases. You will particularly love how the flow effortlessly takes them into designing databases for analytical and AI-centric applications. The book positions you on a path to creating intelligent, data-driven solutions.

Congratulations on getting started on this journey! This book is a strategic companion and hands-on guide for engineers, architects, and developers practicing the art and science of cloud database design.

Bagirathi Narayanan

SVP, Chief Architect, Teladoc Health

Forbes Member Leader

Contributors

About the author

Abirami Sukumaran is a lead developer advocate at Google, focusing on databases and data to AI journey with Google Cloud. She has over 17 years of experience in data management, data governance, and analytics across several industries in various roles from engineering to leadership, and has 3 patents filed in the data area. She believes in driving social and business impact with technology.

She is also an international keynote, tech panel, and motivational speaker, including key events like Google I/O, Cloud NEXT, MLDS, GDS, Huddle Global, India Startup Festival, Women Developers Academy, and so on. She founded Code Vipassana, an award-winning, non-profit, tech-enablement program powered by Google and she run with the support of Google Developer Communities GDG Cloud Kochi, Chennai, Mumbai, and a few developer leads. She is pursuing her doctoral research in business administration with artificial intelligence, is a certified Yoga instructor, practitioner, and an Indian above everything else.

I want to thank Packt and its team along with the tech reviewers for their effort in ensuring that the content is wholesome. My sincere thanks to Martin Paynter (Customer Engineering Manager, Google) and Chris Taylor (VP, Engineering Fellow at Google) for going out of their way to complete the review and approval process smoothly.

About the reviewers

Alfons Muñoz, a dedicated technophile and cloud computing expert, is the Communities Director at C2C, the Google Cloud Customer community. His role involves enriching the GCP professional network through collaboration with Googlers and customers.

Alfons started his Google journey as a partner, specializing in Google Workspace solutions for diverse companies. He holds three Google Cloud certifications, including Google Workspace administrator and Professional Cloud Architect, backed by a B.Sc. in Computer Science. Renowned in the C2C community, Alfons actively engages in global events and conferences, sharing valuable insights into the dynamic world of Google Cloud.

Bitthal Khaitan is a Senior Cloud Engineer at CVS Health, USA. CVS Health is a prominent Fortune #4 healthcare solutions company. With more than 13 years of industry experience, Bitthal has played a pivotal role in driving cloud data-driven initiatives using a versatile technology stack encompassing Google Cloud, Teradata, Big Data, Hadoop, Spark, Scala, and Python. Before his tenure at CVS Health, Bitthal spent eight years at Tata Consultancy Services, Asia's largest IT company as a Data Engineer where he collaborated with Fortune 500 companies like Walmart, Cigna Healthcare, DaVita Kidney Care, and Kaiser Foundation Hospitals on critical projects involving enterprise data warehousing, big data lake development, and cloud migration.

I would like to thank my spouse and my 2 little daughters for being an amazing support system!

Table of Contents

Part 2: Structured Data

3

Database Modeling for Structured Data   29

4

Setting Up a Fully Managed RDBMS   47

10

Looking Ahead – Designing for LLM Applications   177

Preface

This is the age of lightning-speed delivery. Whether it is the physical world of consumer products or the technological world that enables digitization, we want everything developed, built, and delivered at speed and at scale. Yes, I am talking about the software products and applications that are powering several million businesses these days. We all know that the knowledge, design, and choice of the database are critical in that journey. Is there a cookie-cutter template solution that gets you there quickly and correctly? The answer is no. But there are ways to get your idea into a product relatively faster and efficiently with the right design, and technical and business knowledge of your data. That is what I have addressed in this book.

This book focuses on taking the readers on a journey of taking idea through product, with a structured approach to guide you into asking the right questions and knowledge about your own data and business. It will also have a deep-dive discussion on each type and structure of data, and an immersive walk along the entire lifecycle of data in your application. You will also learn about database design best practices, considerations for data security, privacy and compliance with real-world examples and solutions with Google Cloud Database options for each category.

Who this book is for

This book is targeted towards database developers, data engineers, data architects, and data analysts who are looking to build solutions and insights using databases and Google Cloud services tailored to their organizational needs.

What this book covers

Chapter 1, *Data, Databases, and Design*, will help us explore all the basics related to data, database, and modeling. You will learn all the general considerations you need to have while working with them.

Chapter 2, *Handling Data on the Cloud*, will help us dive into the details of cloud computing, and its different types, and explore the use cases and applications. By the end of this chapter, you'll have a clear understanding of cloud computing, its types, use cases, benefits, applications, and considerations.

Chapter 3, *Database Modeling for Structured Data*, discusses structured data, its properties, types, use cases, key considerations, data modeling best practices, SQL basics, and some hands-on data modeling and query experiments.

Chapter 4, Setting up a Fully Managed RDBMS, takes the structured database design to hands-on learning with a fully managed cloud relational database. You will learn how to set up and configure your instance, how to create databases and objects in the database, and how to programmatically connect to the database and access data.

Chapter 5, Designing an Analytical Data Warehouse, will move on to designing for analytical data and take it to hands-on learning with a fully managed cloud data warehouse. You will learn how to set up and configure, create datasets and objects, query, and perform sample analytics on the data.

Chapter 6, Designing for Semi-structured Data, will show you the fundamentals of semi-structured data with examples, real-world use cases, characteristics of semi-structured data, design considerations, and components of a document database.

Chapter 7, Unstructured Data Management, will show you the fundamentals of unstructured data with examples, real-world use cases, how to store, manage, and perform analytics and with unstructured data.

Chapter 8, DevOps and Databases, discusses DevOps and operational attributes of database management like upgrades, security, monitoring, scalability, performance, SLA and SLOs, data federation, CI/CD, migration, and so on. We will also discuss how Google Cloud simplifies the design decisions for these operational considerations.

Chapter 9, Data to AI – Modeling Your Databases for Analytics and ML, explores some key considerations and best practices while designing for analytics, ML, and AI with cloud databases, covering topics like modeling considerations for analytics and ML, analytics, ETL, and the journey of data to AI.

Chapter 10, Looking Ahead – Designing for LLM Applications, will set the stage for data modeling for LLM applications by covering the evolution and basics of LLM, the difference between ML and generative AI applications, the ethical and responsible practices and considerations, and finally the real-world use cases and hands-on implementation to extend your database application to include LLM insights.

To get the most out of this book

Basic understanding of data journey, types, databases, role in the product development cycle, cloud computing, and analytics basics would be useful in getting started with database design and modeling concepts and hands-on implementations.

Software/hardware covered in the book	Operating system requirements
SQL (BigQuery)	Windows, macOS, or Linux
Java 11	
Google Cloud services (on browser): Spanner, Cloud SQL, Firestore, BigQuery, Cloud Storage, Cloud Functions, Cloud Run, Cloud Shell	

If you are using the digital version of this book, we advise you to type the code yourself or access the code from the book's GitHub repository (a link is available in the next section). Doing so will help you avoid any potential errors related to the copying and pasting of code.

If you manage to complete all the exercises in the book, head over to `https://codevipassana.dev` *for more hands-on resources and references.*

Download the example code files

You can download the example code files for this book from GitHub at `https://github.com/PacktPublishing/Database-Design-and-Modeling-with-Google-Cloud`. If there's an update to the code, it will be updated in the GitHub repository.

We also have other code bundles from our rich catalog of books and videos available at `https://github.com/PacktPublishing/`. Check them out!

Conventions used

There are a number of text conventions used throughout this book.

`Code in text`: Indicates code words in text, database table names, folder names, filenames, file extensions, pathnames, dummy URLs, user input, and Twitter handles. Here is an example: "Enter `bigquery-public-data` in the **Type to Search** field again and once it appears, **Expand** this project."

A block of code is set as follows:

```
SELECT country_name, new_confirmed, date, cumulative_confirmed,
population FROM `bigquery-public-data.covid19_open_data.covid19_open_
data` LIMIT 10
```

When we wish to draw your attention to a particular part of a code block, the relevant lines or items are set in bold:

```
SELECT country_name, MAX(cumulative_confirmed) AS TOTAL_CONFIRMED_
COVID19
FROM `bigquery-public-data.covid19_open_data.covid19_open_data`
WHERE cumulative_confirmed > 0
GROUP BY country_name
ORDER BY MAX(cumulative_confirmed) DESC
LIMIT 5;
```

Bold: Indicates a new term, an important word, or words that you see onscreen. For instance, words in menus or dialog boxes appear in **bold**. Here is an example: "To start, click **Activate Cloud Shell from Google Cloud Console** in the top-right corner."

> **Tips or important notes**
> Appear like this.

Get in touch

Feedback from our readers is always welcome.

General feedback: If you have questions about any aspect of this book, email us at `customercare@packtpub.com` and mention the book title in the subject of your message.

Errata: Although we have taken every care to ensure the accuracy of our content, mistakes do happen. If you have found a mistake in this book, we would be grateful if you would report this to us. Please visit `www.packtpub.com/support/errata` and fill in the form.

Piracy: If you come across any illegal copies of our works in any form on the internet, we would be grateful if you would provide us with the location address or website name. Please contact us at `copyright@packtpub.com` with a link to the material.

If you are interested in becoming an author: If there is a topic that you have expertise in and you are interested in either writing or contributing to a book, please visit `authors.packtpub.com`.

Share Your Thoughts

Once you've read *Database Design and Modeling with Google Cloud*, we'd love to hear your thoughts! Scan the QR code below to go straight to the Amazon review page for this book and share your feedback.

`https://packt.link/r/1-804-61145-X`

Your review is important to us and the tech community and will help us make sure we're delivering excellent quality content.

Download a free PDF copy of this book

Thanks for purchasing this book!

Do you like to read on the go but are unable to carry your print books everywhere?

Is your eBook purchase not compatible with the device of your choice?

Don't worry, now with every Packt book you get a DRM-free PDF version of that book at no cost.

Read anywhere, any place, on any device. Search, copy, and paste code from your favorite technical books directly into your application.

The perks don't stop there, you can get exclusive access to discounts, newsletters, and great free content in your inbox daily

Follow these simple steps to get the benefits:

1.   Scan the QR code or visit the link below

https://packt.link/free-ebook/9781804611456

2.   Submit your proof of purchase

3.   That's it! We'll send your free PDF and other benefits to your email directly

Part 1: Database Model: Business and Technical Design Considerations

This part will help you understand the basics of data, database, data modeling, and design. You will learn to use an objective approach to asking the right Business Design and Technical Design Questions. You will also explore a sample application to demonstrate the business and technical aspects.

This part has the following chapters:

- *Chapter 1, Data, Databases, and Design*
- *Chapter 2, Handling Data on the Cloud*

1

Data, Databases, and Design

Data is the foundation of almost all web and mobile applications, and databases are required to handle the essence of your business. There are several database options to choose from, depending on the nature of your business, as well as its type, format, and structure of data, and other design considerations and dependencies of your business and data, on the cloud or otherwise.

Starting with the foundations of databases and design, this book covers fundamentals of database design, data's types, structure, and applications on the cloud, and designing the cloud database model for your application. This will involve us demonstrating database modeling with real-world use cases and examples and integration with other layers of the tech stack like applications, runtimes, analytics and other services such as monitoring, security, access control, analytics, machine learning, and generative AI. The cloud databases and services we will be using to exercise these concepts are all from Google Cloud.

By the end of this book, you'll have learned the fundamentals of cloud database design, taken the data to AI design journey and will have experimented with hands-on applications using Cloud databases and storage options like Cloud SQL, Spanner, Firestore, BigQuery and Cloud Storage. In summary, this book prepares you for designing the data, databases, and data to AI stacks of your product or application with practical examples and hands-on design considerations.

In this chapter, you'll learn about the considerations that are critical in choosing a database at different stages in the life cycle of your data. We will cover the different stages, types, formats, structures and categories of data, types of databases, and the business and technical aspects of database design.

We'll cover the following topics in this chapter:

- Basics of data modeling and design
- Types of data and applications
- Business aspects of data
- Technical considerations
- Types of databases
- Choosing the right database

Data

Raw data can be omnipresent, indefinite, and ubiquitous. Yes – I wake up every day to the smell of freshly ground cardamom as if it were my alarm (my alarm, on the other hand, fails the one job it was designated to do). Anyway, I get ready and drive to work using Google Maps for directions (I like to keep an eye out for traffic, so I choose my routes wisely), log the day's ongoing work for my reference later, check the lunch menu at work in the app, connect with colleagues in Chat (and in person sometimes), work out with my favorite YouTube videos, order food/groceries online, post and connect via social media, and play sleep stories from my meditative collection as I get through and sway my day effortlessly into the non-REM (Rapid Eye Movement, the fourth stage of the sleep cycle) part of my sleep cycle while my subconscious brain starts to pick up where I left off. This cycle repeats as I wake up the next day to the smell of tea and freshly ground cardamom, wondering how nice it would be with some buttery soft sliced bread!

Hmm... if only it weren't for my gluten allergy.

Anyway, the one thing that is half as old as sliced bread but twice as good as that is databases! Imagine the volume and variety of data I share, consume, and involuntarily indulge in throughout my life while undertaking the routine that just I shared (and perhaps I need to get a life)! What goes into accommodating those activities and what resources do I need to accomplish them?

Databases

That's right! The set of application programs that store, access, manage, and update this data while dealing with structure, recovery, security, privacy, concurrency, and more, and attribute comprehensively to getting the day in the life of a modern-day human done right, is the database. It is also called the **database management system** or **DBMS**.

A teeny-tiny bit about the evolution of databases

Long before the term *data* was even coined, humans used the Ishango bone (what is assumed to be a notched baboon bone) as a tally stick speculated to have some mathematical engravings or even something of astrological relevance. Dating to 20,000 years before the present, it is regarded as the oldest mathematical "database" (logging numerical information for future use) tool for humankind, with the possible exception of the approximately 40,000-year-old Lebombo bone from southern Africa. Then, we have Acharya Pingala from the third to second century BC who first described the binary number system that lives on today – forming the foundations of any computing there is, including database systems. Slowly and steadily, we progressed into advanced computing, databases, and technology in general with calculators, computers, automation, wartime wonders, relational database management, the internet, Google Search (yes, it has come to be identified as an important event in the evolution of technology), **artificial intelligence (AI)**, **machine learning (ML)**, and big data.

Isn't it fascinating how everything important dates back to monkeys or monkey bones, just like computers and homo sapiens themselves?

DBMS

Exactly 52 years ago, E.F. Codd, the father of DBMSs, propounded and formalized the 12 commandments, of which there are 13 (starting from 0. I know, right?), that make up a DBMS. You can read about it here: `https://en.wikipedia.org/wiki/Codd%27s_12_rules`. We have evolved since the 1960s, when we used one database to store and secure information, to modern times, where we use one database per stage in the data life cycle – that is, one database per data stage, type, and structure in most cases. We will dive deeper into each of these categories throughout this book with examples and exercises, so don't panic if this is a jargon overdose at this point.

In this chapter, we are going to discuss the business attributes, technical aspects, design questions, and considerations to keep in mind while designing a database model.

Database design

Database design or modeling refers to the activity of designing a database and modeling the data and structure that stores, transforms, manages, and extracts data. Why is it important to design a database so elaborately, you ask? Here are some reasons:

- Data is any organization's most valuable asset and to leverage it to derive the most benefit for the company, we need to ensure it is thoroughly planned and thought through

- As the current generation databases are easy to set up and use, the most common side effect is that business users tend to dive into creating databases with flawed and much-simplified structures without understanding the components of design

- With poorly designed databases, the systems end up having inaccurate results and difficult-to-trace errors, which leads to inconsistent decision-making in the business

If that does not serve your purpose, then consider this: the database is the most critical lifeline of your entire technical architecture as it runs across and connects all the components of your design. It starts with user interfaces, operational systems, messaging services, monitoring systems, analytics solutions, AI/ML applications, and even executive dashboards in the visualization layer that you use for business decision-making. If that lifeline is not well-thought-out, then you are starting your business and technology journey on a path full of surprises, twists, and turns. I understand those are good on paper but very inconvenient when it comes to real-world applications. Imagine having to redesign the foundational component of your understanding 6 months into rolling out your product!

Data modeling

Data modeling is the process of organizing the elements of your data and establishing their relationship with each other and external systems. Within the chosen database environment, a data model represents the structure, attributes (characteristics), relationships, transformations, business rules, and exceptions. There are a lot of data modeling frameworks and tools available in the market, so pick the one that works with your database model, structure of data, business rules, operations, and components of the data.

Database modeling

Database modeling refers to the process of determining the choice and logical structure of your database and designing the way you store, organize, and transform data. I would like to think of a database model as something that needs to be well-vetted out, so that should be the case with the data model. But in a sense, a data model can go through many rounds of trial and error and can evolve as you build compared to a database model, which needs to be designed for scale and also to acclimatize the data model it contains.

Several questions and considerations go into the design and model of a database. That is exactly what we will focus on as a framework in the rest of this chapter.

Considerations for a good database design

Why is it important to take a lot of possible scenarios and probabilities into account while making design decisions? Let me tell you a story that I read in a book called *How Not to Be Wrong*, by Jordan Ellenberg, an interesting read that talks about real-life applications of mathematics.

Like many other things, our story dates back to World War II, when things happened frequently. In this case, the US fighter planes entered combat with loaded machine guns. They didn't want their fighter planes to get shot down by the enemy fighters. So, a **statistical research group** (**SRG**) of extraordinary statisticians was organized to aid the war effort, where equations were developed (and not explosives) to find a solution. Here's the question that was posed to them: "*You don't want the fighter planes to get shot down, so you need to armor them, but armor makes the plane heavier, and heavier planes are less maneuverable and consume more fuel. Not too much, not too little, but we need to armor the planes somewhere at the optimum level.*"

The military gave some useful data to the SRG: when American planes came back from a mission, they were covered in bullet holes. However, the damage wasn't uniformly distributed across the aircraft. There were more bullet holes in the fuselage than in the engines. The bullet-holes-per-square-foot distribution was as follows:

- 1.11 in the engine
- 1.73 in the fuselage

- 1.55 in the fuel system

- 1.8 on the rest of the plane

The officers saw an opportunity to quickly conclude that the armor concentration needed to be in the area with the most bullet holes per square foot. One specific answer from the smartest statistician in that room contradicted this popular opinion, yet it was very insightful. Abraham Wald stated that the armor doesn't go where the bullet holes are the most concentrated, but where they aren't. Wald's insight was simply to ask: where are the missing holes? The missing holes were the ones that would have been all over the engine casing if the bullet hole distribution had been spread equally all over the plane. Wald was sure that the missing holes were on the planes that had been shot down. The officers simply observed the planes that had returned from the mission but the ones that got hit in the engine had not returned at all!

I am sure by now you have already connected the dots as to why it is important to assess all the "missing holes" before you settle on the choice of database and the database model – it is because you don't want to armor the wrong part of your business and end up spending more effort in the long run. If you're wondering whether there is a quick and dirty solution, the short answer is *no*. However, a good design comes with a set of considerations around business attributes and technical aspects while *designing the database model*.

Business aspect

Business requirements are the starting point for your application and also for choosing your database system. There are four stages in the life cycle of data in its business application that help determine the choice of database system:

- Data ingestion

- Storage

- Process

- Visualize

The following diagram represents the attributes in the four stages of data and the categories of questions in each stage in the life cycle of your data:

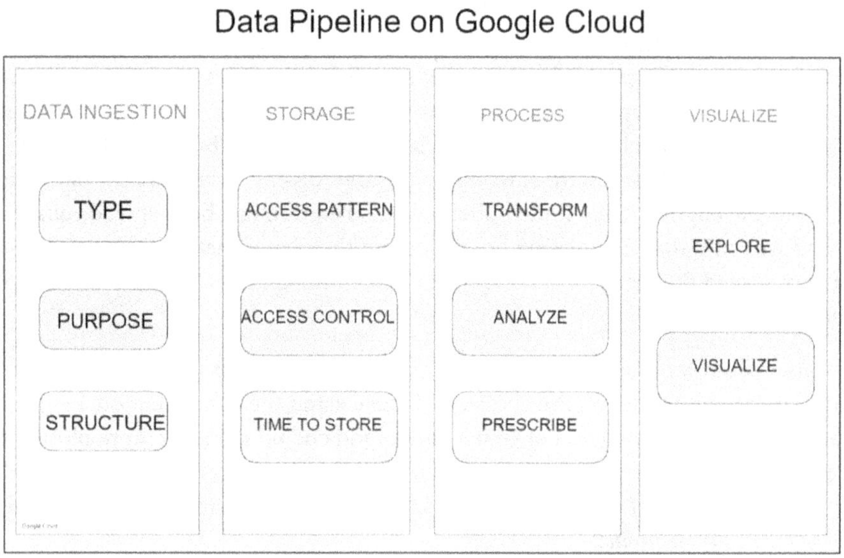

Data Pipeline on Google Cloud

Figure 1.1 – Representation of the four stages of data and the categories of questions in each stage

Let's look at some of these attributes in detail. Some of them are in the business attributes category, while others are technical.

Ingestion

This is the first stage in the data life cycle and it is all about acquiring (bringing in) data from different sources in one place into your system. In this stage, the questions that arise are bucketed into three categories:

- What type of data are you bringing in?
- What is the purpose of this data?
- What is the structure of your data?

Let's take a look at each in detail.

Types of data

There are broadly three types of data we will be dealing with that highly influence the choice of database and storage.

Application data

This is the kind of data that is generated or downloaded as part of the application's content and can contain transactional data that is generated by users and applications – for example, online retail applications, log data from applications, event data, and clickstream data. Let's take a look at a specific example – consider a banking application in which user A transfers money from their account to user B's account. In this case, the user data, such as the account ID, name, bank details, the recipient's name, and transaction date, constitute the application data.

Live stream and real-time stream data

This data comes from real-time sources such as streaming data, which comes in continuously from data sources such as sensor data. These can also be event data responses and can be very frequent compared to batch data processing. It refers to data that is immediately available and not delayed by a system or process. The term *real-time stream* refers to streams of real-time data that are gathered and stored or processed as they come in. This includes monitoring data such as CPU utilization, memory consumption, **Internet of Things (IoT)** devices data such as humidity and pressure, and automated real-time environmental temperature monitoring data.

Batch data

This is data that comes in as bulk at scheduled intervals and could be event-triggered. For example, batch data is transactional data that comes in from applications after a transaction and is stored for use in later stages of the data life cycle. This can include data extracted from one application for use in another at a later point, data migration use cases, and file uploads for processing later. Such applications may not be designed for real-time operations on the data.

The purpose of data

The specific use case and the nature of implementing applications using the data being ingested is a critical factor in determining the choice and design of the database. There may be cases where the type and ingestion mode of data fall into a different choice of database design, whereas its functional use case would imply a different purpose. For example, you could have data streamed in from live events or housekeeping data coming in real-time from transactions, but the specific use case you are designing for might only involve visualization, analytical, or ML functionalities. So, make sure you understand what purpose you are solving with the data that is being ingested in a specific mode and type.

The structure of data

The structure of the data is a crucial factor in deciding the choice and design of a database. There are three widely recognized categories:

- Structured

- Semi-structured

- Unstructured

Let's briefly explore these three categories.

Structured data

This type of data is typically composed of rows and columns; rows are entities or records and columns are attributes. Structured data is organized in such a way that you can be sure that the data structure will be consistent for the most part throughout the life cycle of that data, except for the possible addition or removal of some attributes altogether. This kind of data is mostly transactional or analytical.

Semi-structured data

Semi-structured data does not follow a fixed tabular format – that is, a column-row structure. Instead, it stores schema attributes along with data. The attributes for semi-structured data could vary for each record. The major differentiating factor for each kind of semi-structured data is the way they are accessed.

Unstructured data

Unstructured data includes images, audio files, and so on. Unstructured data does not have a definite schema or data model. The amount of unstructured data is much larger than that of structured data. So, the methods by which we store such data are more important than ever. Here are some examples of unstructured data:

- Text
- Audio
- Video
- Images
- Other **binary large objects (BLOBs)**

Now that we have had a sneak peek into the structure of data, be sure to include functional and design questions based on these categories while designing your database and application model.

Technical aspect

Whether you are engineering or architecting, ask the right data questions! There is always this question about the responsibilities concerning data. When designing data architecture, you must manage the business and technology requirements around the architecture, be involved in designing data extraction, transformation, and loading, and provide direction to the team for methods of organizing, formatting, and presenting data. Once you've done this, you'll be an architect.

As an engineer, you create applications and develop solutions to enable data for distribution, processing, and analysis and participate in one or more of those activities directly.

But in either case, you are an expert. You need to ask the right questions and set the right expectations as you approach the technical aspects of data. It is not always possible to get *the best* solution with the following questions, but they will help you get started and eliminate the mismatches easily right off the bat:

- **Volume and scalability**: Volume is the amount of data you need to store and process in a given period. Scalability is how much you expect your data to grow in the foreseeable future. Here are some questions you can ask in this area:

  - What is the size of data you are going to be dealing with at the time of design and at each stage in the life cycle of the data?

  - How much do you expect it to scale with time?

- **Velocity**: This is the rate at which data is transferred or processed by your application. Some questions that you can ask concerning the velocity of data are as follows:

  - What is the rate/schedule at which the data needs to be sent and processed?

  - If you are ingesting, processing, and writing into storage, do you need to match the velocity at each of these stages?

- **Veracity**: Veracity is the amount of variation you can expect in the data structure and attributes:

  - What variation is expected to be seen in the incoming data?

- **Security**: Access control, encryption, and security are key considerations at the database design stage:

  - How much access restriction (row-level, object-level, and fine-grained levels of access control), encryption, privacy, and compliance does your data need?

  - What kind of encryption is required for the data?

  - Do you need to design views based on the type of data and access control required for your data?

  Other common areas of design consideration are availability, resilience, reliability, and portability.

- **Data retrieval**: Data can be retrieved in many different modes, depending on your use case. The design aspects to keep in mind concerning retrieval are as follows:

  - What is the volume of the data being read?

  - What is the volume of the data being written?

  - What is the frequency of reads?

  - What is the frequency of writes?

This is a key technical aspect to address in design because when it's not done in design, often, engineers and architects are posed with performance challenges and go back to assessing their foundational architecture and configuration at a much-matured stage in development.

Choosing the right database

Having assessed all these questions and considerations, the logical next step is to choose from/eliminate from the database types out there, predominantly focusing on the structured and less structured types of data:

- Relational databases:

  - **Online transaction processing (OLTP)**

  - **Online analytical processing (OLAP)**

- NoSQL databases:

  - Document database

  - Key-value database

  - Wide-column database

  - Graph database

Let's look at these different categories. We will see some examples of some of these categories in the next chapter.

Relational database

The first category we are going to look at is the relational database. There are two broad categories of relational databases: OLTP and OLAP systems.

Online transaction processing

We have the good old relational database for OLTP, which typically follows these normalization rules:

1. **First normal form**: Each column in the table has atomic value, contains no duplicates, and contains a primary key, which is one or more ordered columns that uniquely identify a row.

2. **Second normal form**: A relation is in the second normal form if the first normal form is satisfied and a separate table is used to store all the values that apply to multiple rows and linked using foreign keys. A foreign key is one or more ordered columns that relate to a primary key in another table.

3. **Third normal form**: A relation is in the third normal form if the second normal form is satisfied and if the column that is transitively dependent on the primary key should be eliminated and moved to another table, along with the determinant. So, if attribute A is the primary key, A is dependent on B, and B is dependent on C, then A to C form transitive dependency. So, the dependency between B and C should be moved to a different table.

Transactional structured data is usually operated one row at a time. For example, consider an application where you are looking up employee information. In this case, you will need a lot of attributes (columns) from a single row. So, it is efficient to store all row attributes together and retrieve them in a block. This is what is called **row-oriented storage**.

Online analytical processing

OLAP is typically used for data mart and data warehouse applications. This type requires **Structured Query Language** (**SQL**) to define, manipulate, query, and manage. They usually facilitate the following:

- Aggregations and roll-ups
- Drill down
- Pivots
- Slicing and dicing

For example, imagine a scenario where your business or data analyst needs to retrieve reporting summaries such as total employees joined in the last month and total cost to the company incurred. In this case, you will only query three columns. So, for all the rows selected, instead of retrieving all the columns, it makes sense to only retrieve three. This is a common pattern in analytical applications, and they use a **column-oriented storage** mechanism.

NoSQL database

There are NoSQL databases for semi-structured data – that is, data less structured than fully structured tabular data. There are a few types of NoSQL databases. There is no formal model or normalization requirement for this type.

Sometimes, it's misleading when we hear that NoSQL options are schema-less. NoSQL options may not have a schema in the same pattern as relational databases, but they do have a structure to represent data. Four broad types of NoSQL databases are loosely based on a specific way of storing data. Let's look at the logic for a data model in each case.

Document database

A document database stores data in document format, similar to a JSON document. Each document stores pairs of fields and values, with a wide variety of data types and data structures used as values. Document databases allow you to keep adding attributes as needed without making changes to the database schema each time.

For example, consider the scenario where you cannot fix all the attributes at the design stage and have to add more attributes as the process evolves, such as in the case of a retail store selling electronic equipment where a laptop has memory, a processor, a charger, and other configuration attributes and a washing machine has another set of attributes, such as weight, power, length, width, and so on. To search efficiently by these attributes, document databases allow for indexes. If you want to search an equipment by length, then you can create an index on length.

Key-value database

The key-value model consists of a key and a value, and it is the simplest type of database in terms of understanding and usage. The data model has two parts: data and a string associated with the data. Data can be accessed via direct request (send the key and get the data) rather than using any kind of query language. Key-value databases are simple if you have to search only on your key. However, if your value-data structure is complex, for example, a JSON object is stored as a value, and if you want to be able to search on items within the JSON structure, then a key-value database is not the best option. In that case, a document database would be a better option.

The following table is an example of a key-value database:

Key	Value
Key1	Value1
Key2	Value2
Key3	Value1
Key4	Value3

Table 1.1 – Key-value example table

Let's discuss key-value databases next.

Wide-column database

Wide-column databases follow a table form structure that is both flexible and scalable. Each row has a key and one or more associated columns, called column families. Each row's key-column family is allowed to have as many numbers of columns and the columns can have as many kinds of data as possible. Data is accessed using a query language. This type of column structure allows for faster summary (aggregation) queries. Wide-column databases are designed in such a way that they respond to specific queries. Instead of using indexes to allow efficient lookup of rows, wide-column databases store data in such a way that rows with similar keys (row keys are like primary keys in relational databases) are close together.

For example, consider log data from an application. The following table represents data that is organized to answer queries looked up by event ID and then time:

Event ID	Time	Description
1	5431023867	Event successful
2	5431023869	Error looking up…
3	5431023868	Finished with error

Table 1.2 – Table organized by Event ID and Time

The preceding table is not applicable for querying events in the past hour because it is not organized by time first. The following table, on the other hand, is organized to answer queries by time range. Note that a new table with the desired schema needs to be created to accomplish this. Wide-column databases do not use indexes for queries:

Time	Event ID	Description
5431023867	1	Event successful
5431023868	3	Finished with error
5431023869	2	Error looking up…

Table 1.3 – Table organized by Time and Event ID

Let's move on to graph database next.

Graph database

Graph databases consist of nodes and edges. Nodes are connected by edges. Data is stored in the nodes and information about how the nodes are related is stored in the edges. Node and edge data is typically retrieved using query languages, **Graph Query Language** (**GQL**), and sometimes SQL as well. There are two types of query methods we can use to retrieve data from graph databases:

- Cypher Query Language, which specifies SQL-like statements that describe patterns in a graph
- Traversal Language, which specifies how to navigate from one node to another in the graph

People and connections are a great example of a use case for graph databases. A person could be designed as the node and the relationship of that person with other persons could be the links, also known as edges.

In the following diagram, persons 1, 2, 3, 4, 5, and 6 are all people and the link between them denotes *friends*:

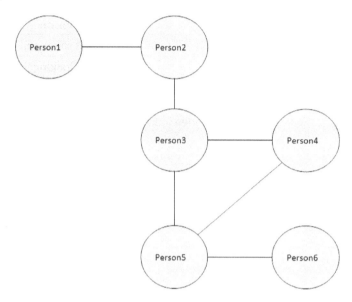

Figure 1.2 – Representation of nodes and edges in a graph database

We will look into some of these categories in detail later in this book. For now, let's summarize what we've learned in this chapter.

Summary

Data and databases form the core of any system, product, process, application, and even idea these days. Also, there are a lot of them lately. So, choosing the one that fits your needs and adds value, precision, cost-effectiveness, and representation to your information is paramount. This chapter aimed to point you in the direction of the right questions to ask at the time of design and modeling. As you possibly already know, almost always drive business with technology and not the other way around. Make the right database choices and data design decisions in a way that works for you.

In the upcoming chapters, we will look into some of these categories in detail with hands-on examples while also providing how-to guides and best practices. Before that, we will look at cloud computing and basics of handling data on cloud in the next chapter.

2
Handling Data on the Cloud

What is cloud computing? By definition, it is the idea of getting things done with someone else's computer. Have you noticed that little cloud-shaped icon in the "shapes and icons" collection in word editors that we use to represent the internet, in our flow charts and architecture diagrams? That is where it started. The idea of hosting any service on the internet became known as **cloud computing**, inspired by the icon. Cloud computing was created to accommodate the exponentially growing volumes of data, resources, and services that organizations use, which has been causing more expense and a lot of maintenance effort for several decades now. It is the kind of technology where we store, process, maintain, and visualize applications and data and other dependencies in a central, managed environment, basically with someone else's resources (the provider who hosts and manages).

In this chapter, we'll dive into the details of cloud computing, its different types, and explore its use cases and applications. By the end of this chapter, you'll have a clear understanding of cloud computing.

In this chapter, we'll cover the following topics:

- The types of cloud services
- Use cases
- The benefits of cloud computing
- Data applications on cloud
- Managed, unmanaged, and database as a service
- Cloud database considerations

You may think these topics sound quite theoretical. The first couple of chapters are mainly to create a foundation and get all the basic concepts out of the way, allowing you to enjoy the real-world use cases with hands-on exercises in the upcoming chapters. Just bear with me for a few more topics, and then we'll dive right into practical database design.

Types of cloud services

Cloud services are divided into three main types:

- A **public cloud** provides open and accessible public services on the internet. It is a cloud computing service that provides computing resources, such as virtual machines, storage, and networking, over the internet to multiple customers or users. It is operated and maintained by a cloud service provider and is made available to the public on a pay-as-you-go or subscription basis.

- A **private cloud** provides hosted services to a private group of people, mostly within an organization, with access restrictions and permissions in place in terms of infrastructure, network, and data. Unlike public clouds, which serve multiple customers, a private cloud is dedicated to a single tenant. It can be hosted on-premises within an organization's own data center or infrastructure, or it can be hosted by a third-party provider off-site. This is preferred when organizations require greater control, security, and customization over their cloud infrastructure, particularly in situations where sensitive data and regulatory compliance are major concerns.

- A **hybrid cloud** is a combination that uses both public and private clouds. For example, organizations can run sensitive, mission-critical applications on private cloud services and use public services for other workloads and demands that are not sensitive in nature. The advantage of this type of cloud is that it unifies the workloads between the private and public clouds, allowing automation and the use of infrastructure and data between the two, while preserving the sensitivity of the applications that require it.

In addition to all this, we have organizations that look for a multi-cloud option. This enables them to integrate and migrate applications between different clouds, working as if they coexisted in terms of concurrency, access, and so on.

Use case categories

Use cases are divided broadly into three main categories:

- **Infrastructure as a Service** (**IaaS**) is based on a model where the infrastructure that the organization needs is rented, but virtually. In the IaaS model, cloud service providers deliver fundamental IT infrastructure components, including virtual machines, storage, and networking, to users on a pay-as-you-go basis.

  With IaaS, organizations can offload the management and maintenance of physical hardware and data centers, allowing them to focus on building and managing their applications and services. Users have the flexibility to scale resources up or down based on their specific needs, making it an ideal choice for businesses with variable workloads or those seeking cost-effective solutions.

- **Platform as a Service** (**PaaS**) is based on a model where the platform for development, designing, and deploying software applications is offered without having to worry about the server, storage, maintenance, security, scaling, load balancing, and so on.

PaaS offerings include not only infrastructure components but also tools, services, and development frameworks that streamline the application development process. PaaS is particularly well suited for software developers and development teams who want to build scalable and agile applications. It offers tools for collaboration, continuous integration, and continuous deployment, making it easier to manage the entire application life cycle.

- **Software as a Service** (**SaaS**) is a model that delivers applications directly for use totally on demand, without you having to worry about downloading or installing files, software, or applications. Just accessing the site via a browser would do. These applications are hosted and maintained by cloud providers, relieving users of the burden of software installation, maintenance, and updates.

  One of the key benefits of SaaS is its scalability and ease of adoption. Organizations can quickly add or remove user licenses as needed, and updates and improvements are automatically delivered by the provider. This eliminates the need for extensive IT support and reduces upfront software licensing costs. SaaS offers a wide range of software solutions, including productivity tools (e.g., email and office suites), **customer relationship management** (**CRM**) systems, collaboration platforms, and industry-specific applications.

This can be better represented with the following diagram:

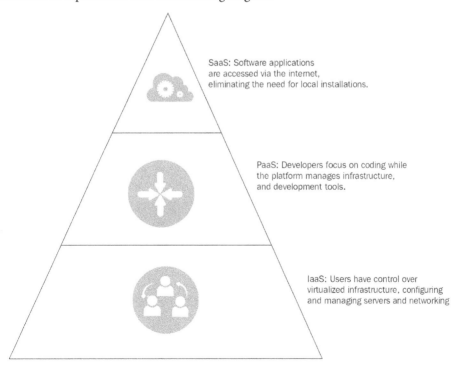

Figure 2.1 – A classification of use cases

Now that we have looked at the broad classification by use cases, let's dive further into their applications.

The benefits of cloud computing

There are numerous benefits to cloud computing. Let's look at a few of the most important ones to our topic:

- **Ease of use**: The programs and applications (in the case of SaaS) are exclusively managed by vendors, and you do not need to worry about how to run an application.

- **Customization**: Even updates to existing applications have become easy, with SaaS involving a point-and-click method and no need to change code extensively.

- **Pay-as-you-go**: You pay only for what you use and can terminate or pause services at any time.

- **Avoiding the cost of infrastructure**: Build and deploy applications without worrying about the cost of compute and other resources, such as servers, operating systems, and networks.

- **Pay only for what you need**: You choose what you want to use and pay only for those features and services, depending on the service, and you do not have to be concerned about paying for anything else.

- **Upgrades and updates**: You can fully rely on the cloud services to take care of all your maintenance, upgrades, updates, and other tracking tasks.

- **Elastic scaling**: Depending on your growing needs, your resources may grow past your initial assessment. Cloud services handle this automatically without causing disruption or downtime to your applications. Most services allow you to scale down to nothing when not in use.

- **Service-level agreements**: You will get a guaranteed uptime and performance of your applications and services with cloud providers' service-level agreements, for each service as applicable.

- **Self-service**: Users can start their own compute resources on demand, without having to rely on an operations or administration team to provision and manage it all for them.

- **Resilience**: Cloud computing promises resilience and continuity of business by implementing the redundancy of resources across regions (as applicable) for storage, availability, and so on.

- **Ease of migrations**: Organizations often encounter changes in the implementation of solutions, in terms of workload shift or architectural shift, for better cost and performance. Cloud computing makes it relatively easier for them to migrate workloads and services across cloud platforms and on-premise to the cloud, without having to heavily involve an extended team of operations and administration.

- **Multi-tenancy**: Since data is all on the cloud logically (even though physically stored somewhere), several users can share resources in terms of infrastructure and applications, with the assurance that their data is kept private and secure.

So far, we have learned about the fundamentals of the cloud, the different types, their use cases, and their benefits. In the upcoming sections, we will see how they can be applied in the data and database realm with real-world applications and considerations.

Data applications on cloud

Storing information on the cloud allows you access from anywhere with internet connectivity. It allows data to scale up or down exponentially with elasticity. This is the main advantage for any organization migrating to the cloud because, this way, they can focus on ideas and innovation for business transformation and agility, rather than worrying about data management and infrastructure to support that. Let us take a look at some areas of application for data on the cloud in this section.

Storage

Cloud computing manages storage and access for organizations' data in any format – files, audio, video, images, tables, documents, and so on. The need and application to have a storage area that can be accessed from anywhere on any device at any time (as per the agreed service-level agreements) are critical these days for all businesses across industries. Cloud providers also support this with easy-to-use interfaces that allow interactive access and configuration of the stored information.

Backup and disaster recovery

Safe data backup is critical for organizations because of the possible permanent loss of data if there is a disaster. Cloud computing offers backup and storage right from the get-go, and it also enables easy recovery and even point-in-time and minimal-to-zero damage at times of disaster. Support for multi-region backup and availability is also extended, based on the privacy regulations and standards for the business in its region.

Analytics and insights

This is the most common application to handle data on the cloud. There is always room and need for data visualization, analysis, analytics, insights, prediction, and prescription across all businesses and industries. For all this, organizations need extremely large volumes, velocity, and variety of data, also known as **big data**, which is ideal for a cloud computing use case because of the unlimited storage capacity and scale that cloud services offer and support.

Application development

Cloud computing offers several services for easy application development, testing, and deployment. Conventionally, we used to have an infrastructure team or operations team that enabled this pipeline. This involved resources, infrastructure, time, and manpower. But with the cloud, these can be mostly self-serviced, and teams can focus on developing their product and innovating toward the growth and development of their business. The journey from code check-in to deploying an app and rolling out the product in the cloud, all at the click of a button, is the power of handling data on the cloud for application development.

User experience and personalization

Customer experience and personalization are two important aspects of customer satisfaction in any business. Particularly in business use cases (e.g., banking, e-commerce, and education), storing data on the cloud enables you to make a lot of decisions and apply insights to personalize services to each user individually. Besides that, it also offers the power to keep sensitive information private and secure, valuing individual preferences and anticipating customers needs. These aspects set a business ahead of its competition. Cloud environments are ideal for areas that involve customer data, product data, marketing, and other operational data and insights.

These are some of the real-world applications of handling data on the cloud. In the following section, we will look into the different ways you can handle data on the cloud.

Managed, unmanaged, and database as a service

Handling data on the cloud involves storage and access, and this is enabled using databases. It is not a one-size-fits-all choice. There are several options and criteria to make the right database choice for your application and product, which we discussed in detail in *Chapter 1, Data, Databases, and Design* of this book. In this section, let us look at the managed and unmanaged types of database categories.

Managed databases

When your team needs to focus more on creating an application and product rather than focusing on operations and maintenance, you need a solution or a service that gives you those capabilities by shifting the infrastructure, maintenance, and latency requirements to the cloud provider. That is exactly what a managed database provides.

Managed databases provide users the ability to maintain clusters, routine updates, scalability, backup, recovery, replication, latency, availability, and administration in a very self-sufficient and cost-effective way. They are built to support some of the following features but are not limited to just these:

- Version maintenance (minor version automation)
- Retention, replication, backup, and recovery
- Scalability
- Automated clustering as applicable
- Availability
- Access control and security
- Resilience and flexibility

All of these and many more advantages come with having your databases fully managed by the provider. There are definitely use cases and real-world applications that benefit from this method of dealing with data.

Unmanaged databases

An unmanaged database is the kind where all the aforementioned features and more are not taken care of by the provider, and you are required to provision them on your own. When your requirements demand you to place the all the responsibility for support, maintenance, and setup on your developer, infrastructure, or operations teams, you would need to turn to the database installed as part of your application framework or initial setup. The entire list of actions, including installation, maintenance, upgrades, monitoring, reliability, and security, all fall under the responsibilities of your teams, and these actions could become time-consuming, slow, and exposed to vulnerabilities. However, there are situations that drive this kind of requirement. Some of them are listed here:

- Advanced data regulatory, sovereignty, and privacy requirements

- Private network or firewall requirements

- Unavailability of support for the required database or operating systems from cloud providers

- Non-production environments

- Out-of-scope requirements in terms of size, variety, and operations

With time, the need for unmanaged databases is narrowing only to selective domains or industries that have such strict regulatory requirements, which force them to manage systems on their own. Having said that, some scenarios, such as the need for extreme customization and flexibility, the maintenance of legacy systems, specific cost restrictions, classified government applications, healthcare or finance systems, and, in some cases, even the need for a specialized database or configurations that are not readily available as managed services, make it imperative to use unmanaged databases.

Database as a service

Database as a service is a managed database service that adheres to SaaS principles to a certain extent – that is, enabling a database application as a service to several customers via API provisioning and so on, without time needing to be spent configuring or managing the database. This means it is more ready-made than managed databases. The service isolates customers in terms of data, encryption, clusters, compute, and so on.

Let's take a quick glance at the three types of database services in this table of differences:

Feature	Managed	Unmanaged	Database as a service
Deployment and maintenance	Fully managed	Self-managed	Fully managed
Infrastructure	Fully managed	Self-managed	Fully managed
Provisioning and scaling	Fully managed	Self-managed	Fully managed
Patching and upgrades	Fully managed	Self-managed	Fully managed
Backup and recovery	Fully Managed	Self-managed	Fully managed
Monitoring and alerts	Fully managed	Self-managed	Fully managed
Security	Built-in security features	Self-managed	Built-in security features
Customization and control	Flexible but limited	Full	Very limited
Expertise required	Minimal	High	Minimal
Cost	Mostly usage-based	Infrastructure, management, and resource cost	Subscription and usage-based

Table 2.1 – The difference between managed, unmanaged, and database as a service

Now that we have covered the differences and properties of the different ways of handling data, let's move on to considerations that enable the choice of database.

Cloud database considerations

There are a few considerations when we decide to move to cloud databases. The previous chapter covered the various business, technical, and design considerations you must go through before choosing the right database for your application or business. Here, we want to address a few more cloud-specific aspects to keep in mind while approaching a cloud database design:

- **Security, regulations, privacy, and compliance**: Security is the most important software design and delivery factor, and it sometimes can pose a challenge as well, depending upon the nature of the data and the complexity of your requirements. Teams and organizations should pay attention to cloud security standards, configurations, regulatory requirements for their product, regional (geo-specific) requirements, encryption features and stages, business policies, and other best practices and guidelines.

- **Cost**: Even though we have established that you only pay as you go or pay per use for services as applicable, we also have to remember that cost can fluctuate with your scaling workload needs. This makes it less predictable if not strategized properly. For example, if you anticipate having a social media influencer advertise your application or product in the next three months or so, plan to accommodate the anticipated increase in cost, owing to the increase in web traffic in terms of page visits and even actionable transactions on your page during this time period. It is not always possible to plan all the other factors contributing to an increase in traffic or cost over a period of time, without observing the usage and history of transactions and user behavior for a time range. Consider involving descriptive, predictive, and prescriptive analytics to get the most out of your database design.

- **Resources and expertise**: With the availability of multiple services and cloud providers, it is possible to struggle with a mismatch in skillsets, resources, tools, and technologies. Making design decisions based on the workload, nature, and the business and technical requirements of your organization is already a pivotal task. In addition to that, you should also consider the skillset and availability of your resources, providing training requirements on demand for the choices you make.

- **Data governance**: With fully managed cloud databases, you get the privilege and capability of doing it all yourself, but this can quickly obstruct data governance and management guidelines. There is a very limited need to control provisioning and management with cloud-managed databases, which can lead to data quality, governance, and security challenges, and even risks. It is important to place a strong emphasis on evaluating governance needs when it comes to design so that teams are aware of the restrictions and best practices, and incorporate them at the configuration stage to prevent any late-stage impact on the quality of data or database processes.

- **Migration, lock-in, and flexibility**: When you make design decisions and choices about cloud databases and services, make sure you also evaluate for flexibility when moving data, schema, other services, and applications between clouds, from the public to the private cloud, or even from one cloud provider to another. Migration can sometimes incur very long processes and expenses if not evaluated for flexibility and ease of implementation at the design stage. It is more often than not overlooked and later ignored because of the unplanned cost it poses at a much later stage, resulting in poor performance or low-quality applications and solutions for your data and business. Also, keep in mind that there could be legal and regulatory issues, if not evaluated properly, for specific migrations, due to vendor-specific lock-in requirements that were overlooked at the design stage.

These considerations, in addition to cloud provider data center locations, multi-region replication capabilities, integration with third-party tools and other cloud services, data transfer, and egress costs, are crucial in determining the right cloud database that aligns with your specific requirements, offering the services that best suit your needs.

A quick follow-up

Remember, in the last chapter, when we discussed the different database categories and decided to defer discussing examples of each of those categories to the following chapter? Let's address that here! So, now that you know what cloud computing is and the role it plays in handling data and applications, we should be able to look at cloud database examples for each type:

- Relational database:

  - **Online Transaction Processing (OLTP)**: Spanner, Cloud SQL, and Alloy DB

  - **Online Analytical Processing (OLAP)**: BigQuery

- NoSQL database:

  - **Document database**: Firestore

  - **Key-value database**: Memorystore

  - **Wide-column database**: Bigtable

  - **Graph database**: JanusGraph

We will discuss some of these databases in detail with real-world use cases, hands-on exercises, and design practices in the upcoming chapters of this book.

Summary

Now that we have discussed what cloud computing is, and its implications, types, ways of handling data on the cloud, use cases that determine those methods, real-world applications, and considerations to make the right choice for your data requirements, you should be in a better position to design a robust, scalable, and cost-efficient cloud database infrastructure that meets the needs of your applications and users. However, before that, you should learn about the various data formats, the different types databases to handle that data and the real-world applications, hands-on. The following chapter is a short introduction to structured data, its database design considerations, its applications, and the Google Cloud options with real world use-cases and hands-on implementations that inform your design.

Part 2:
Structured Data

This part details the characteristics of structured data. We will also explore the database options available in Google Cloud for structured data. Moving ahead, we will do a deep dive into Cloud SQL, Cloud Spanner, and BigQuery.

This part has the following chapters:

- *Chapter 3, Database Modeling for Structured Data*
- *Chapter 4, Setting Up a Fully Managed RDBMS*
- *Chapter 5, Designing an Analytical Data Warehouse*

3
Database Modeling for Structured Data

In this chapter, we will discuss the properties, types, use cases, and key considerations of structured data, data modeling best practices, and SQL basics, and we will look at some hands-on data modeling and query experiments.

In this chapter, we'll cover the following topics:

- Structured data
- RDBMS for structured data
- Considerations for your RDBMS
- Structured query language

Structured data

Structured data is data that has a well-defined structure, type, and format organized and standardized in a repository called a **database** for storage, retrieval, and processing. **Structured Query Language** (**SQL**) is used for interacting with this data. This means that structured data has a fixed set of attributes and is in the format of rows and columns.

Rows and columns

Rows are the entities or records and columns are attributes. Simply put, columns are the labels or headers in your table and rows are the values under those headers. Consider *Table 3.1*:

Name	Age	ZIP
John Doe	35	33306
Michael Angel	40	33309

Table 3.1 – A table with rows and columns

The **Name**, **Age**, and **ZIP** labels are the column names, while the values associated with them, including **John Doe** and **Michael Angel**, are rows. Data that's in a structured format is typically associated with transactional and analytical applications.

Transactional applications

Transactional applications are those where the operation is mostly done one record at a time. Transactional applications may include use cases such as lookup, commit, submit, validate, modify, and search. Here are some examples of transactional applications:

- A banking application where data that's sent and received is processed
- A shipping application where customer addresses are looked up
- An attendance application where a student's attendance status is marked

In these kinds of applications, many or all columns from a single record will be accessed for a transaction. So, the ideal way to store them for performance and efficiency is in blocks of data so that retrieving a block will result in all associated data being retrieved. This is common in transactional databases, which follow row-oriented storage.

Analytical applications

Analytical applications are those that consolidate, aggregate, and summarize structured data for analysis. This kind of application may include use cases such as describe, predict, forecast, prescribe, aggregate, and cumulate. Here are some examples of analytical applications:

- Customer engagement metrics
- Usage analytics
- Sales forecast applications
- Marketing analytics

In these kinds of applications, the end user is only interested in fields that relate to the summarized information – for example, date, monthly sales, annual revenue, and monthly use activation. So, instead of getting all the fields for each record, it is ideal to store and retrieve only those columns that are relevant to the application. This is common in analytical databases, which follow column-oriented storage.

Using an RDBMS for structured data

A **Relational Database Management System** (**RDBMS**) is a type of database management system that stores data in a structured format, allowing relationships to be made with other data stored within the database while adhering to the **Atomicity, Consistency, Isolation, and Durability** (**ACID**) properties of all transactions. Let's take a look at these properties.

Atomicity

This property means that the transactions are completed in a manner that ensures that all the changes to data are complete or none of them are. For example, if an application transfers money from *Account A* to *Account B*, and if the debit from *Account A* is successful, then it is assumed that *Account B* will be credited with the money being transferred.

Consistency

This property means that data is in a consistent state throughout the life cycle of the transaction. For example, in the transaction we spoke about in the previous example, if the state of the transaction is collectively the same – that is, the total value of the transaction remains the same at the start and end of the transaction – then the transaction is considered consistent.

Isolation

This property means that the state of a transaction is not visible to another transaction until it is entirely complete. For example, in the transaction we have been discussing, when transferring funds from Account A to B, the transferred fund is seen in A or B but not in both and not in neither.

Durability

This property means that the state of the transaction is permanent after it is successful. For example, in the transaction we have been discussing, once the transfer is successful, there is no reversal of the transaction, even if there is a system disaster.

By adhering to the ACID properties, an RDBMS ensures the reliability and integrity of data, even in the event of a system failure. Apart from these fundamental four properties, there are also other properties of an RDBMS, such as referential integrity, data independence, security, scalability, and more. We will briefly cover these in the upcoming section.

Considerations for your RDBMS

There are some considerations and best practices for RDBMS modeling. Here are some of these key considerations:

- **Purpose, functionality, type, and structure**: The first step in data modeling is to understand the business requirements. What data do you need to store? How will the data be used? What is the type, structure, and purpose of the data you are dealing with? Once you understand the business requirements, you can start to design the data model.

- **Entities and attributes for the use case**: The next step is to identify the entities and attributes in the data model. Entities are the basic building blocks of a data model. They represent real-world objects or concepts. Attributes are the properties of entities. They describe the characteristics of entities.

- **Relationship and dependency of entities and attributes**: Once you have identified the entities and attributes, you need to define the relationships between entities. Relationships are the connections between entities. They show how entities are related to each other.

- **Usage of appropriate data types**: Choose data types that accurately represent the nature of the data and its expected values. Avoid using excessively large data types that can lead to wasted storage and diminished query performance. Additionally, use appropriate constraints to enforce data integrity.

- **Data profiling in terms of outliers, anomalies, and potential data quality issues**: Start with a comprehensive understanding of your data. Profile your structured data thoroughly to identify outliers, anomalies, and potential data quality issues. This step lays the foundation for accurate modeling by ensuring that your data is clean, consistent, and representative of the real-world scenario it depicts.

- **Data normalization requirement**: Only you can decide the right normalization needs and constraints for your data, depending on the access type, frequency, and purpose of your applications. Strive for the right balance between normalization and denormalization. While normalization reduces redundancy, denormalization enhances query performance. Consider the specific usage patterns and query requirements of your data when deciding on the optimal level of normalization.

- **Indexing strategy for faster data retrieval**: Identify the most frequently queried columns and create indexes accordingly. However, be cautious not to over-index, as this can impact write performance. Regularly monitor and fine-tune indexes as data usage patterns evolve.

- **Horizontal and vertical scaling/partitioning strategy**: When dealing with large datasets, consider partitioning your data. Partitioning involves dividing a table into smaller, more manageable segments. This approach enhances query performance as it allows the database engine to focus on relevant partitions instead of scanning the entire dataset.

- **Query optimization**: Optimize your queries by structuring them efficiently and utilizing the power of database query optimization tools. Minimize the use of wildcard characters in WHERE clauses, use joins judiciously, and consider using stored procedures to encapsulate complex queries for reusability and performance gains.

- **Caching mechanisms for frequent reads**: Implement caching mechanisms to reduce the load on your database. Use in-memory caching solutions to store frequently accessed data, reducing the need for repeated database queries. This technique can significantly enhance response times and improve overall system performance.

- **Ease of setup and access**: The RDBMS you choose should be easy to set up and use for both developers and other users directly or indirectly. Make sure you assess all your high-level functional and non-functional requirements and build/run as many prototypes/tests as required to make an informed decision. Use realistic test datasets and representative workloads to gauge the impact on both precision and performance. This practice helps you avoid unforeseen issues in a production environment.

- **Scalability, performance, and future-proofing**: Design your data architecture with scalability in mind. Leverage cloud-native solutions and distributed databases that can handle growth seamlessly. Consider horizontal scaling options and prepare for data volume increases without compromising performance.

- **Security, encryption, and access control**: There are some critical aspects in the areas of security and access control for your data: robust authentication mechanisms (such as strong passport policies, **multi-factor authentication** (**MFA**), and integration with external identity providers), granular access control, data encryption at rest and in transit, data access audit and monitoring capabilities, data masking, row-level access security, vulnerability assessment, and backup and recovery security. You need to ensure the database choices and modeling assessments you are performing cover these primary capabilities as part of the offering.

- **Replication**: It is important to ensure you have a proper replication strategy for your data at the time of modeling your database. While preparing for it, make sure you evaluate the latency and synchronization needs, consistency requirements (strong, eventual, and so on), conflict resolution mechanism, automatic failover strategy, minimum downtime needs, read-write scalability, network, monitoring, and diagnostic needs, backup and restore policies, and more for your use case. By evaluating these replication considerations, you'll be well-equipped to choose an RDBMS and create a model that aligns with your data distribution, availability, scalability, and consistency requirements.

- **Integration flexibility**: With your data needs, you will also have a wide variety of integration requirements and external dependencies. It is important to design and prototype for these during the data modeling phase to ensure the data dependencies and any other organizational or use-case-specific integrations are possible with the database of your choice.

The ideal choice of RDBMS should be a result of assessing these factors concerning your application. It is important to consider these attributes during data modeling to ensure that your data model is designed in a way that takes advantage of the strengths of the RDBMS you choose and minimizes its weaknesses.

But how can we talk about structured data and not discuss SQL or write some queries? We'll do that next.

Structured query language

SQL is the protocol that's used to access, query, and interact with data in your RDBMS. It is common because of the simplicity of performing even advanced data operations and analysis. There are a few main forms of SQL:

- **Data Definition Language** (DDL): This is a language that lets you define structures and make changes to the schema, tables, constraints, and more. Examples include `create`, `alter`, `truncate`, `drop`, and `rename` statements.

- **Data Manipulation Language** (DML): This language lets you manipulate data in your database. There are four major operations involved in this – **Create, Read, Update, and Delete** (CRUD). Examples include `insert`, `update`, and `delete` statements.

- **Data Query**: This is a type of statement that lets you query data and extract results for the desired analysis. An example is a `select` statement.

- **Data Control Language** (DCL): This is the language that lets you control access to data in your database in terms of authorization. Examples include `grant`, `deny`, and `revoke` statements.

Most relational databases support ANSI-compliant SQL.

Sample SQL queries

Here are some examples of SQL queries:

- `SELECT * FROM PRODUCTS;`

- `SELECT * FROM PRODUCTS WHERE PID = 100;`

- `UPDATE PRODUCTS SET PRODUCT_NAME = 'table' where PID = 100;`

Since we won't be spending much time focusing only on SQL in this book, I wanted to use this section to solidify the basics of SQL. If you are an analyst or a database developer who's familiar with these queries, you can extend these use cases to more complex SQL applications.

Shall we make this SQL immersion a little hands-on? Consider each of the following real-world scenarios and craft your best responses to them. Also, feel free to attempt the SQL queries in your favorite database/data warehouse, with modifications to the SQL constructs if needed.

> **Note**
>
> Please be advised that certain features and services described in the following sections may have undergone modifications since writing this chapter. The screenshots may look different from what you see in the book. APIs and versions may have been updated at the time you are reading this. As such, kindly exercise flexibility and adapt your steps accordingly.
>
> Additionally, some services may incur charges if they are outside the free tier (if applicable). Therefore, it is recommended to be aware of the services you are enabling and to delete or deactivate services and instances that are no longer required for learning or demonstration purposes.

In this case, I am going to take BigQuery as my choice of data warehouse. The BigQuery sandbox lets you explore limited BigQuery capabilities at no cost to confirm whether BigQuery fits your needs. The BigQuery sandbox lets you experience BigQuery without the need for a credit card or creating a billing account for your project. If you've already created a billing account, you can still use BigQuery at no cost in the free usage tier:

1. Open the BigQuery console by entering the following URL in your browser: `https://console.cloud.google.com/bigquery`.

2. Authenticate yourself with your Google account or create one.

3. Enter the necessary details – **Country**, **Terms of Service**, and other options – and click **AGREE AND CONTINUE**.

4. Create your project by entering its name, organization (no organization in this case), and region.

5. You will be taken to the BigQuery console, and you'll see a message stating that you have successfully enabled **SANDBOX**. Dismiss it and get started.

In the BigQuery console that opens, you should see the **Explorer** pane on the left and **SQL Workspace** on the right, as shown in the following screenshot:

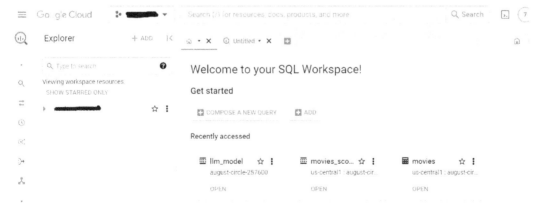

Figure 3.1 – The BigQuery console

Open a new SQL **Editor** tab and try out the use cases.

Make sure you have a dataset created in BigQuery (or if you are not using BigQuery, have an instance and database created). In this case, I have created a dataset named db_model. Some of the queries in this section may have to be modified according to the database/warehouse product you are choosing. For example, in the DDL statements, STRING(255) in BigQuery will be represented as VARCHAR(255) or VARCHAR2(255) in some other product. The NOT ENFORCED keyword may have to be removed if you're not using BigQuery.

Let's look at the sample use cases and SQL statements now.

Use case 1

Imagine you're designing a database for an e-commerce platform.

Data model: How would you structure your database to efficiently manage products, categories, and customer orders?

- **Answer**: The DDL for creating the tables is as follows (this has been provided as a guideline only; you may need to change it according to your database):

```
-- Products table
CREATE OR REPLACE TABLE db_model.products (
    product_id INT PRIMARY KEY NOT ENFORCED,
    product_name STRING(255),
    category_id INT,
    price DECIMAL(10, 2)
);

-- Categories table
CREATE TABLE db_model.categories (
    category_id INT PRIMARY KEY NOT ENFORCED,
    category_name STRING(255)
);

-- Orders table
CREATE TABLE db_model.orders (
    order_id INT PRIMARY KEY NOT ENFORCED,
    customer_id INT,
    order_date DATE
);

-- Order Items table
CREATE TABLE db_model.order_items (
    order_item_id INT PRIMARY KEY NOT ENFORCED,
```

```
        order_id INT,
        product_id INT,
        quantity INT
);
```

- Here's how you can insert data into these tables:

```
-- Insert sample data into products table
INSERT INTO db_model.products (product_id, product_name,
category_id, price)
VALUES
    (1, 'Laptop', 1, 899.99),
    (2, 'Smartphone', 1, 499.99),
    (3, 'Smart TV', 2, 799.99);

-- Insert sample data into categories table
INSERT INTO db_model.categories (category_id, category_name)
VALUES
    (1, 'Electronics'),
    (2, 'Home Appliances');

-- Insert sample data into orders table
INSERT INTO db_model.orders (order_id, customer_id, order_date)
VALUES
    (1, 101, '2023-08-15'),
    (2, 102, '2023-08-16');

-- Insert sample data into order_items table
INSERT INTO db_model.order_items (order_item_id, order_id,
product_id, quantity)
VALUES
    (1, 1, 1, 2),
    (2, 1, 2, 1),
    (3, 2, 3, 3);
```

SQL question: Provide a SQL query to retrieve the two top-selling products in a specific category:

- **Answer**:

```
SELECT p.product_name, COUNT(o.order_id) AS sales_count
FROM db_model.products p
JOIN db_model.order_items oi ON p.product_id = oi.product_id
JOIN db_model.orders o ON oi.order_id = o.order_id
JOIN db_model.categories c ON p.category_id = c.category_id
WHERE c.category_name = 'Electronics'
```

```
GROUP BY p.product_name
ORDER BY sales_count DESC
LIMIT 2;
```

Let's look at a different use case.

Use case 2

Our next use case revolves around a social media application.

Data model: How would you structure your database to handle user posts, comments, and likes?

- **Answer**:

```
-- Users table
CREATE TABLE db_model.users (
    user_id INT PRIMARY KEY NOT ENFORCED,
    username STRING(255)
);

-- Posts table
CREATE TABLE db_model.posts (
    post_id INT PRIMARY KEY NOT ENFORCED,
    user_id INT,
    post_content STRING,
    post_date TIMESTAMP
);

-- Comments table
CREATE TABLE db_model.comments (
    comment_id INT PRIMARY KEY NOT ENFORCED,
    post_id INT,
    user_id INT,
    comment_content STRING,
    comment_date TIMESTAMP
);

-- Likes table
CREATE TABLE db_model.likes (
    like_id INT PRIMARY KEY NOT ENFORCED,
    post_id INT,
    user_id INT,
    like_date TIMESTAMP
);
```

- Here's how we can insert the necessary data into these tables:

```
-- Insert sample data into users table
INSERT INTO db_model.users (user_id, username)
VALUES
     (1, 'user1'),
     (2, 'user2'),
     (3, 'user3');

-- Insert sample data into posts table
INSERT INTO db_model.posts (post_id, user_id, post_content,
post_date)
VALUES
     (1, 1, 'Hello, world!', '2023-08-15 10:00:00'),
     (2, 2, 'This is my first post.', '2023-08-16 14:30:00');

-- Insert sample data into comments table
INSERT INTO db_model.comments (comment_id, post_id, user_id,
comment_content, comment_date)
VALUES
     (1, 1, 2, 'Nice post!', '2023-08-15 10:30:00'),
     (2, 1, 3, 'Welcome!', '2023-08-15 10:45:00');

-- Insert sample data into likes table
INSERT INTO db_model.likes (like_id, post_id, user_id, like_
date)
VALUES
     (1, 1, 3, '2023-08-15 11:00:00'),
     (2, 2, 1, '2023-08-16 14:35:00');
```

SQL question: Provide a SQL query to retrieve the two latest posts, along with the total number of comments and likes for each post:

- **Answer**:

```
SELECT p.post_id, p.post_date, p.post_content,
COUNT(c.comment_id) AS comment_count, COUNT(l.like_id) AS like_
count
FROM db_model.posts p
LEFT JOIN db_model.comments c ON p.post_id = c.post_id
LEFT JOIN db_model.likes l ON p.post_id = l.post_id
GROUP BY p.post_id, p.post_date, p.post_content
ORDER BY p.post_date DESC
LIMIT 2;
```

Let's move on to the next use case.

Use case 3

Suppose you're designing a database for a library.

Data model: How would you model books, authors, and borrowers?

- **Answer**:

```
-- Books table
CREATE TABLE db_model.books (
    book_id INT PRIMARY KEY NOT ENFORCED,
    title STRING(255),
    author_id INT
);

-- Authors table
CREATE TABLE db_model.authors (
    author_id INT PRIMARY KEY NOT ENFORCED,
    author_name STRING(255)
);

-- Borrowers table
CREATE TABLE db_model.borrowers (
    borrower_id INT PRIMARY KEY NOT ENFORCED,
    borrower_name STRING(255)
);

-- Loans table
CREATE TABLE db_model.loans (
    loan_id INT PRIMARY KEY NOT ENFORCED,
    book_id INT,
    borrower_id INT,
    loan_date DATE
);
```

- Here's the data we need to insert into these tables:

```
-- Insert sample data into books table
INSERT INTO db_model.books (book_id, title, author_id)
VALUES
    (1, 'The Great Gatsby', 1),
    (2, 'To Kill a Mockingbird', 2),
    (3, '1984', 3);

-- Insert sample data into authors table
```

```
INSERT INTO db_model.authors (author_id, author_name)
VALUES
    (1, 'F. Scott Fitzgerald'),
    (2, 'Harper Lee'),
    (3, 'George Orwell');

-- Insert sample data into borrowers table
INSERT INTO db_model.borrowers (borrower_id, borrower_name)
VALUES
    (101, 'Alice Johnson'),
    (102, 'Bob Smith');

-- Insert sample data into loans table
INSERT INTO db_model.loans (loan_id, book_id, borrower_id, loan_
date)
VALUES
    (1, 1, 101, '2023-08-15'),
    (2, 2, 102, '2023-08-16');
```

SQL question: Provide a SQL query to find the most borrowed book, along with its author:

- **Answer**:

```
SELECT b.title AS book_title, a.author_name, COUNT(l.borrower_
id) AS borrow_count
FROM db_model.books b
JOIN db_model.authors a ON b.author_id = a.author_id
JOIN db_model.loans l ON b.book_id = l.book_id
GROUP BY b.title, a.author_name
ORDER BY COUNT(l.borrower_id) DESC
LIMIT 1;
```

Let's explore the final use case in this chapter.

Use case 4

Imagine you're building a database for an online music streaming service.

Data model: How would you structure your database to handle songs, artists, and user playlists?

- **Answer**:

```
-- Songs table
CREATE TABLE db_model.songs (
    song_id INT PRIMARY KEY NOT ENFORCED,
```

```
        song_title STRING(255),
        artist_id INT
);

-- Artists table
CREATE TABLE db_model.artists (
    artist_id INT PRIMARY KEY NOT ENFORCED,
    artist_name STRING(255)
);

-- Playlists table
CREATE TABLE db_model.playlists (
    playlist_id INT PRIMARY KEY  NOT ENFORCED,
    playlist_name STRING(255),
    user_id INT
);

-- Playlist Songs table (to associate songs with playlists)
CREATE TABLE db_model.playlist_songs (
    playlist_id INT,
    song_id INT,
    PRIMARY KEY (playlist_id, song_id) NOT ENFORCED
);

-- Plays table (to track song plays)
CREATE TABLE db_model.plays (
    play_id INT PRIMARY KEY NOT ENFORCED,
    song_id INT,
    user_id INT,
    play_date TIMESTAMP
);
```

- We must insert the following data into these tables:

```
-- Insert sample data into songs table
INSERT INTO db_model.songs (song_id, song_title, artist_id)
VALUES
    (1, 'Song A', 1),
    (2, 'Song B', 2),
    (3, 'Song C', 1);

-- Insert sample data into artists table
INSERT INTO db_model.artists (artist_id, artist_name)
VALUES
```

```
     (1, 'Artist X'),
     (2, 'Artist Y'),
     (3, 'Artist Z');

-- Insert sample data into playlists table
INSERT INTO db_model.playlists (playlist_id, playlist_name,
user_id)
VALUES
     (1, 'My Favorites', 101),
     (2, 'Party Mix', 102);

-- Insert sample data into playlist_songs table
INSERT INTO db_model.playlist_songs (playlist_id, song_id)
VALUES
     (1, 1),
     (1, 2),
     (2, 3);

-- Insert sample data into plays table
INSERT INTO db_model.plays (play_id, song_id, user_id, play_
date)
VALUES
     (1, 1, 101, '2023-08-15 14:00:00'),
     (2, 2, 102, '2023-08-16 16:30:00');
```

SQL question: Provide a SQL query to list the two most popular songs by play count:

- **Answer**:

```
SELECT s.song_id, s.song_title, a.artist_name, COUNT(p.play_id)
AS play_count
FROM db_model.songs s
JOIN db_model.artists a ON s.artist_id = a.artist_id
JOIN db_model.plays p ON s.song_id = p.song_id
GROUP BY s.song_id, s.song_title, a.artist_name
ORDER BY COUNT(p.play_id) DESC
LIMIT 2;
```

Try running these queries yourself with additional data if you like and analyze the query's response.

Just a few quick reminders:

- You may have to change the data types in a way that is acceptable for your database of choice – mainly, you may have to replace STRING with VARCHAR in some databases and remove the NOT ENFORCED keyword.

- Try building data models and answering those queries in your own way, keeping in mind that the database model, objects, and dependencies you are building are going to impact the core functioning, performance, and precision of the applications and businesses for which you are designing this data model.

- Please note that these DDL statements provide a basic structure for each use case, and you would need to add constraints, indexes, and other elements as required by your specific application and database system. Additionally, these statements don't include foreign key constraints or data types for all columns, which would be important in a production database.

Alright, let's move on from the use cases to some core constructs of SQL. Now, since it is not the only focus of this book, I am not going to get into all the details of it, but I am going to quiz you with some conceptual SQL questions that can get you started if you are an absolute beginner or if you are a seasoned data practitioner who likes to engage in these kinds of exercises:

1. What is the difference between a SELECT and DELETE statement?

   • A SELECT statement is used to retrieve data from a database, while a DELETE statement is used to delete data from a database.

2. How do you use a JOIN statement to combine data from two tables?

   • A JOIN statement is used to combine data from two tables by matching the values of common columns. There are three types of JOIN statements: INNER JOIN, LEFT JOIN, and RIGHT JOIN.

3. How do you use a GROUP BY statement to group data by a common value?

   • A GROUP BY statement is used to group data by a common value. The GROUP BY statement can be used with the SELECT statement to retrieve the aggregated results of the query.

4. How do you use an ORDER BY statement to sort the results of a query?

   • An ORDER BY statement is used to sort the results of a query. The ORDER BY statement can be used with the SELECT statement to sort the results of the query by one or more columns.

5. How do you use a WHERE clause to filter the results of a query?

   • A WHERE clause is used to filter the results of a query. A WHERE clause can be used with a SELECT statement to filter the results of the query based on the values of one or more columns.

6. How do you use subqueries to nest queries within queries?

   • A subquery is a query that is nested within another query. Subqueries can be used to perform complex queries that would be difficult or impossible to perform with a single query.

7. How do you use views to create virtual tables?

    • A view is a virtual table that is created from one or more tables. Views can be used to simplify complex queries or provide a security layer for your database.

8. How do you use triggers to automate database operations?

    • A trigger is a special type of stored procedure that is executed when a particular event occurs in the database. Triggers can be used to automate database operations, such as updating a table when a new record is inserted into another table.

9. How do you use stored procedures to encapsulate database logic?

    • A stored procedure is a block of SQL code that is stored in the database. Stored procedures can be used to encapsulate database logic, making it easier to maintain and reuse your code.

10. How do you use functions to create reusable expressions?

    • A function is a special type of stored procedure that returns a value. Functions can be used to create reusable expressions, making it easier to write complex queries.

11. How do you use window functions to aggregate data over a group of rows?

    • Window functions are a type of function that can be used to aggregate data over a group of rows. Window functions can be used to calculate running totals, moving averages, and other aggregations.

12. How do you use **common table expressions** (CTEs) to improve the readability and performance of your queries?

    • CTEs are a way to temporarily store the results of a query in a virtual table. CTEs can be used to improve the readability and performance of your queries by breaking them down into smaller, more manageable chunks.

13. How do you use JSON functions to work with JSON data in your database?

    • JSON functions are a set of functions that can be used to work with JSON data in your database. They can be used to parse JSON data, extract data from JSON, and update JSON data.

14. How do you use XML functions to work with XML data in your database?

    • XML functions are a set of functions that can be used to work with XML data in your database. They can be used to parse XML data, extract data from XML data, and update XML data.

15. How do you use partitioning to improve the performance of your queries?

    • Partitioning is a way to divide a table into smaller pieces. Partitioning can be used to improve the performance of your queries by isolating hot spots and by allowing you to parallelize queries.

16. How do you use recursive CTEs to create self-joins?

   • Recursive CTEs can be used to create self-joins, which are joins between a table and itself. Recursive CTEs can be used to implement complex queries that would be difficult or impossible to implement with other types of joins.

17. How do you use materialized views to improve the performance of your queries?

   • Materialized views are a type of view stored in the database. Materialized views can be used to improve the performance of your queries by caching the results of a query.

18. How do you use distributed queries to process data across multiple servers?

   • Distributed queries are queries that can be processed across multiple servers. Distributed queries can be used to process large amounts of data or to improve the performance of queries that would be too slow to run on a single server.

19. How do you use encryption to secure your data in the database?

   • Encryption can be used to secure your data in the database by protecting your data from unauthorized access, modification, or disclosure. Make sure your choice of database or data warehouse service has encryption at rest and in transit, which means that your data will be encrypted while in storage or transaction.

20. How do you use auditing to track changes that have been made to your data?

   • Auditing can be used to track changes to your data. It can also be used to identify unauthorized access, modification, or disclosure of your data. Make sure your choice of database or warehouse has monitoring, auditing, and related features available. Cloud storage options in general take care of this and most of them are fully managed.

Okay – let's say you got all of those questions right. If you'd like some more challenges, go ahead and consider those four use cases we covered right before these questions to create some SQL queries on your own that incorporate the database constructs and objects covered in these conceptual questions.

Summary

In this chapter, we comprehensively covered structured data, its properties, types, real-world use cases, some key considerations, and best practices for data modeling for structured data. We explored SQL basics, provided examples of SQL queries for various use cases, including e-commerce, social media, library, and music streaming platforms, and demonstrated how SQL queries can efficiently retrieve relevant data from structured databases.

Throughout this chapter, hands-on scenarios and SQL challenges were presented, encouraging you to apply your knowledge of data modeling and SQL to real-world use cases. In the next few chapters, we will look at some of these Google Cloud databases for structured data in detail with real-world hands-on use cases.

4

Setting Up a Fully Managed RDBMS

In the previous chapter, we discussed the considerations and best practices when designing a database for storing structured data, and some real-world SQL examples. In this chapter, we will take the structured database design to do some hands-on learning with a fully managed cloud relational database. You will learn how to set up and configureyour instance, and create databases and objects in the database and how to programmatically connect to the database and access data.

In this chapter, we'll cover the following topics:

- Fully managed databases
- Fully managed RDBMS
- Cloud SQL as an example
- Setting up and configuring a fully managed RDBMS
- Creating an application with the cloud database
- Operational aspects of cloud relational databases

Fully managed databases

Fully managed databases reduce the need for manual effort and lower the costs involved in administering your databases. They also allow your teams to focus more on productive areas of work, contributing to your business. In a fully managed database, the provider takes care of infrastructure provisioning, maintenance, routine updates, scalability, backup, recovery, replication, latency, availability, security, privacy, regulatory settings, and administration in a very self-sufficient and cost-effective way, as opposed to self-managed databases, where all of these need to be done by the database administration teams.

Some examples of self-managed databases are the non-cloud version of MySQL, PostgreSQL, SQL Server, Maria DB, Oracle, and IBM DB2. Some of these databases have equivalent managed cloud services..

Fully managed RDBMS

A fully managed **Relational Database Management System** (**RDBMS**) is a provider-managed database system that does the following:

- Structures data in tables made of rows and columns

- Has the ability to join tables to derive information between related data

- Adheres to the **atomicity, consistency, isolation, and durability** (**ACID**) properties of your applications' transactions

- Supports integrity constraints to maintain data consistency across multiple tables

- Supportive of rows having a unique identifier, columns have unique names, and values are atomic

- Has values that all have the same datatype in a given column

- Has a fixed schema definition for the relational data model, and the **data definition language** (**DDL**) changes for any further schema-level modifications

Let's dive into the setting up, configuration, and application of the most preferred fully managed cloud relational database service for MySQL, PostgreSQL, and SQL Server databases, and Cloud SQL.

Cloud SQL

Cloud SQL is a fully managed database service that makes it easy to set up, maintain, manage, and administer your relational databases on the Google Cloud Platform. It supports up to 99.99% availability and supports up to 64 TB of storage, with the ability to automatically increase storage size as needed. You can use Cloud SQL with MySQL, PostgreSQL, and SQL Server.

As we already discussed, Cloud SQL is a fully managed database and Google will take care of all operational activities including minor version upgrades, backup, recovery, scaling (if user configures for it), failover, monitoring, authorization, networking, security, observability, and so on. The following are some of its key features:

- Cloud SQL provides integration to other Google Cloud services such as Cloud Run, GKE, Cloud Functions, BigQuery, and Compute Engine

- It has secure access

- It has high availability with its zonal/regional database replication feature

- It can scale up by adding more memory, processing, storage, and so on, and scale out with highly available read replicas for high read traffic

- Its monitoring tools and Query Insights feature aid root cause analysis and offer the option to integrate with existing monitoring tools

- It supports performance-heavy workloads with very high input/output operations per second

- Its real-time change data capture feature allows for recovery and data syncing with minimal latency

- Its automated daily backup and point-in-time recovery allow instance restoration to a specific point in the past

- Its API support allows you to set up, build, and deploy programmatically with standard connection drivers and built-in migration tools

For a list of detailed features, refer to the Google Cloud documentation for Cloud SQL: `https://cloud.google.com/sql#section-2`.

In the following section, we will see how to maintain your MySQL relational database on Google Cloud with Cloud SQL.

> **Note**
>
> Please be advised that certain features and services described in the following sections may have undergone modifications since the time of drafting. The screenshots may look different from what you see in the book. APIs and versions may have been updated by the time you are reading this. As such, kindly exercise flexibility and adapt your steps accordingly.
>
> Additionally, some services may incur charges if they are outside the free tier (if applicable). Therefore, it is recommended to be aware of the services you are enabling and to delete or deactivate services and instances that are no longer required for learning or demonstration purposes.

Setting up and configuring a fully managed RDBMS

If you are new to Google Cloud, go to the Google Cloud console (`https://console.cloud.google.com/`), select your organization, and create a new Google Cloud project with billing enabled.

You can follow the instructions here:

`https://cloud.google.com/resource-manager/docs/creating-managing-projects`.

All the steps mentioned in the following subsections can be done with Cloud Shell commands or via the Google Cloud console.

Creating a Cloud SQL instance for MySQL

Go to the Google Cloud console and, in the search bar, search for `Cloud SQL`. Then, follow these steps:

1. Go to the Cloud SQL instance page at `https://console.cloud.google.com/sql`. The following figure shows the Cloud SQL instance page:

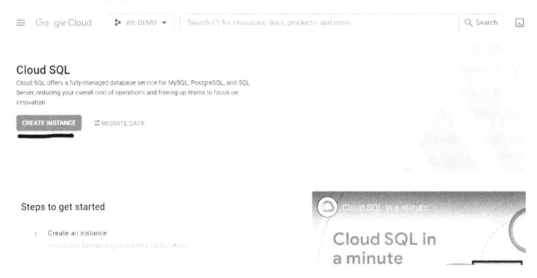

Figure 4.1 – The Cloud SQL instance page

2. Click on the **CREATE INSTANCE** button. This will take you to the **Create an instance** page, as shown here:

Figure 4.2 – The Create an instance screen

3. Click **Choose MySQL** and enable the Compute Engine API by clicking the **ENABLE API** button if it prompts you to do so, as shown in the following figure:

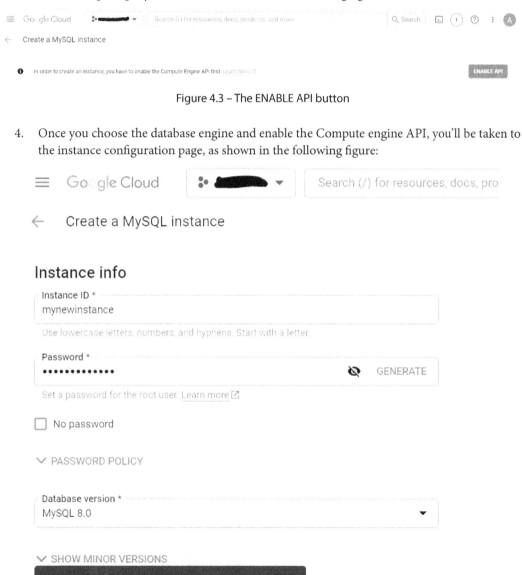

Figure 4.3 – The ENABLE API button

4. Once you choose the database engine and enable the Compute engine API, you'll be taken to the instance configuration page, as shown in the following figure:

Figure 4.4 – The instance configuration page

5. Enter a valid unique name for **Instance ID**.

6. Enter a root password.

7. For the purposes of this demo, I have chosen a Cloud SQL edition of Enterprise and Sandbox. Choose the one that works for your needs. The Enterprise Plus option gives you a 99.99%-availability SLA, high-performance machines, and a broader timeline for point-in-time recovery.

8. Choose the region, memory, storage, and zonal availability configuration per your needs.

9. Expand the **Customize your instance** section and validate your storage, connections, data protection, and instance delete protection configurations.

> **Note**
>
> If you leave the **Enable instance delete protection** checked, you will not be able to delete it after completing the demo. But this feature is really handy to prevent accidental instance deletion for production applications.

10. Finally, click **Create**.

Once the instance is created, you will be taken back to the instances list and you should be able to see the newly created instance.

Connecting to the instance

We will use Cloud Shell commands to connect to the instance we just created:

1. Go to the Google Cloud console and click the **Cloud Shell** icon, circled in red here:

Figure 4.5 – The Cloud Shell icon

2. You should be able to see the terminal with the welcome message, as shown in the following screenshot:

Figure 4.6 – The cloud terminal

3. At the prompt, enter the `connect` command as shown here. Make sure to replace `<<instance_ name>>` with the instance you created in the previous section:

```
gcloud sql connect <<instance_name>> --user=root
```

In this case, the instance name is `mynewinstance`:

```
gcloud sql connect mynewinstance --user=root
```

If it prompts you to enable `sqladmin.googleapis.com`, type `y` and hit Enter, as shown in the following screenshot:

```
Welcome to Cloud Shell! Type "help" to get started.
Your Cloud Platform project in this session is set to ▇▇▇.
Use "gcloud config set project [PROJECT_ID]" to change to a different project.
▇▇▇▇▇▇▇$ gcloud sql connect mynewinstance --user=root
API [sqladmin.googleapis.com] not enabled on project ▇▇▇. Would you like to enable and retry (this will take a few minutes)? (y/N)?  y

Enabling service [sqladmin.googleapis.com] on project ▇▇▇...
Operation "operations/acat.p2-188868830713-760eb247-3911-424b-b61a-abc81a39d64a" finished successfully.
```

Figure 4.7 – Enabling sql.admin.googleapis.com

4. Click **Authorize** when you are prompted to authorize Cloud Shell.

5. Enter the root password when prompted.

> **Note**
> If the instance is created and you skipped creating a password for root, you can always update it after creating the instance, as shown in the following figure:

Figure 4.8 – Changing the root password

Now you are connected to the instance, you should see the `mysql` prompt, as shown here:

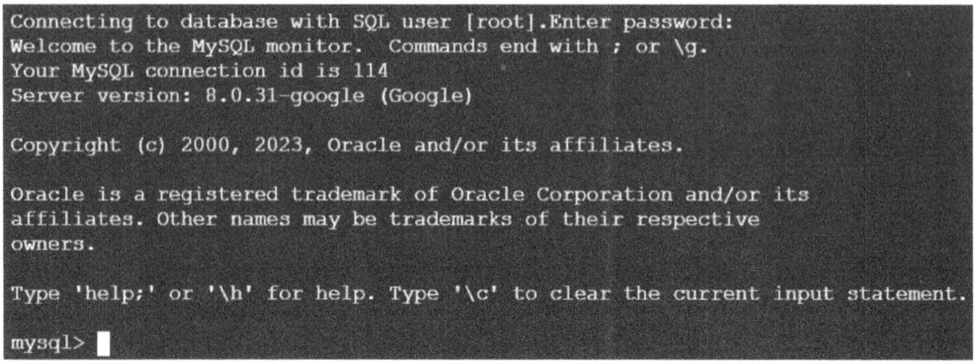

```
Connecting to database with SQL user [root].Enter password:
Welcome to the MySQL monitor.  Commands end with ; or \g.
Your MySQL connection id is 114
Server version: 8.0.31-google (Google)

Copyright (c) 2000, 2023, Oracle and/or its affiliates.

Oracle is a registered trademark of Oracle Corporation and/or its
affiliates. Other names may be trademarks of their respective
owners.

Type 'help;' or '\h' for help. Type '\c' to clear the current input statement.

mysql>
```

Figure 4.9 – MySQL prompt

Let's now create the database.

Creating a database

We will continue in the Cloud Shell terminal to create a database. You can create a database on the Cloud SQL for MySQL instance using the following command:

```
CREATE Database <<database_name>>;
```

In this case, we'll use the following command:

```
CREATE Database test_db;
```

This should create a database named `test_db` in the `mynewinstance` instance, as shown here:

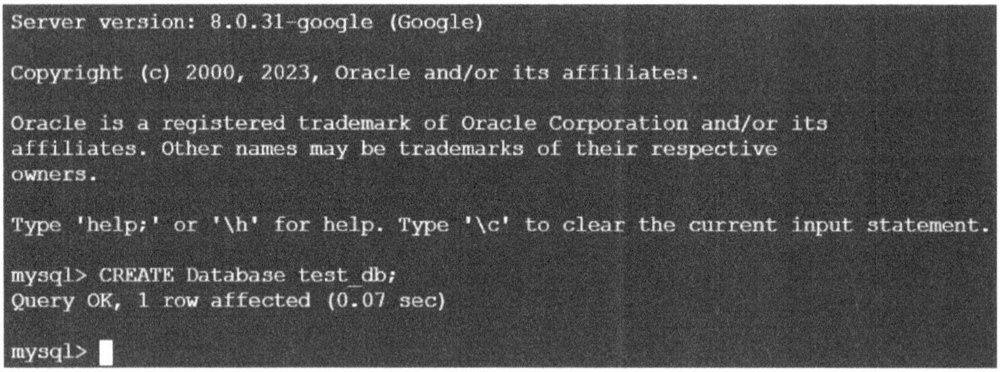

```
Server version: 8.0.31-google (Google)

Copyright (c) 2000, 2023, Oracle and/or its affiliates.

Oracle is a registered trademark of Oracle Corporation and/or its
affiliates. Other names may be trademarks of their respective
owners.

Type 'help;' or '\h' for help. Type '\c' to clear the current input statement.

mysql> CREATE Database test_db;
Query OK, 1 row affected (0.07 sec)

mysql>
```

Figure 4.10 – Creating the test_db database

Next, let's create a table.

Creating a table

You can use the following command to create a table in the newly created database:

```
Use <<database_name>>
CREATE TABLE <<table_name>>(
  <<column1>> INT NOT NULL AUTO_INCREMENT,
  <<column2>> <<datatype>>,
  PRIMARY KEY(<<column1>>)
  );
```

Replace `<<table_name>>`, `<<column N>>`, and `<datatype>>` with their respective values.

In this case, our DDL is as follows:

```
CREATE TABLE test_db.test_table (
  index_column INT NOT NULL AUTO_INCREMENT,
  string_column VARCHAR(255),
  PRIMARY KEY (index_column)
);
```

This should create a table called `test_table` in the `test_db` database we created, as seen in the following figure:

```
mysql> CREATE TABLE test_db.test_table (
    ->     index_column INT NOT NULL AUTO_INCREMENT,
    ->     string_column VARCHAR(255),
    ->     PRIMARY KEY (index_column)
    -> );
Query OK, 0 rows affected (0.09 sec)
```

Figure 4.11 – Creating the test_table table

Let's insert values into the `test_db` table now.

Inserting values

You can insert sample data into a table using the following SQL command:

```
INSERT INTO <<table_name>> (<<column2>>) VALUES (<<value2>>);
```

In our case, the query is as follows:

```
INSERT INTO test_db.test_table VALUES (1, 'This is a test 1');
```

Let's insert one more row. Since we have AUTO_INCREMENT set on the index_column field, you can insert values into the string_column field using the following SQL statement:

```
INSERT INTO test_db.test_table(string_column) VALUES ('This is a test
2');
```

This automatically increments the index_column field corresponding to the data as 2 since our last inserted value is 1.

The following screenshot shows the result after both of the inserts:

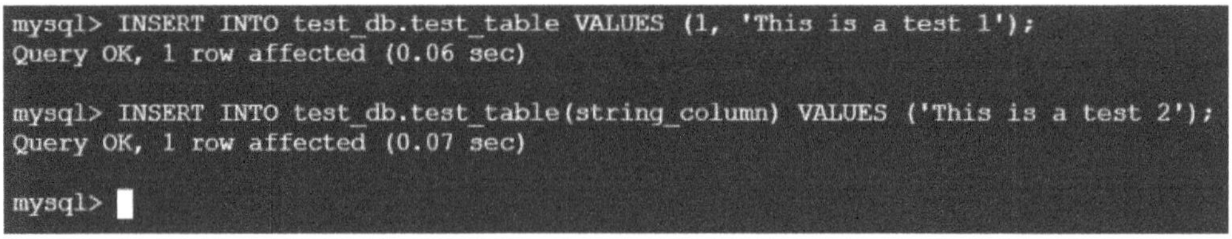

```
mysql> INSERT INTO test_db.test_table VALUES (1, 'This is a test 1');
Query OK, 1 row affected (0.06 sec)

mysql> INSERT INTO test_db.test_table(string_column) VALUES ('This is a test 2');
Query OK, 1 row affected (0.07 sec)

mysql>
```

Figure 4.12 – The output of the insert statements

Now, let's view the data.

Querying values

Let's query the data we just inserted:

```
SELECT * FROM <<table_name>>;
```

In our case, the table name is test_table:

```
SELECT * FROM test_db.test_table;
```

You should see the following result: 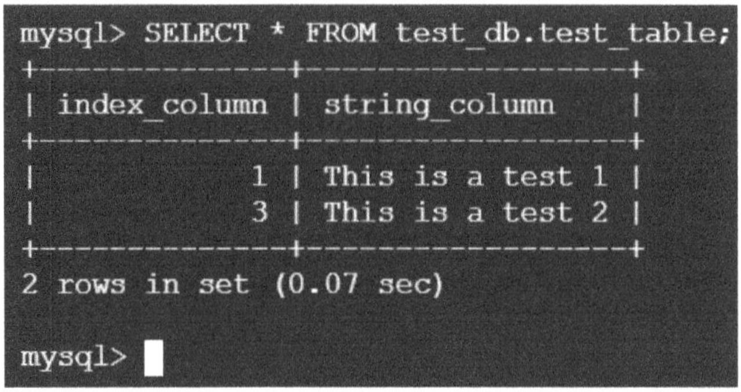

```
mysql> SELECT * FROM test_db.test_table;
+--------------+---------------+
| index_column | string_column |
+--------------+---------------+
|            1 | This is a test 1 |
|            3 | This is a test 2 |
+--------------+---------------+
2 rows in set (0.07 sec)

mysql>
```

Figure 4.13 – Querying the table values

Yay! We have created a Cloud SQL for MySQL instance, a relational database, and a table and inserted a few values into them.

Creating an application with the Cloud database

Let us create a small one-page application to see how to access Cloud SQL for MySQL programmatically. You can try it in any programming language of your choice. I am going to use Java as my preferred language for code samples.

Before stepping into the application, make sure you have the Cloud Functions service account configured for Cloud SQL connections.

Configuring the Cloud Functions service account

Perform the following steps to configure your Cloud Functions service account:

1. Go to the Google Cloud console's IAM page using this link: `https://console.cloud.google.com/iam-admin/iam`.

2. Edit the service account – **Compute Engine default service account** – to add a role.

3. Click on **Add another role**.

4. Add the **Cloud SQL Client** role.

5. Click **Save**.

Now that the service account is configured, let's create the functions.

Creating a Cloud Function

Cloud Functions let you create and deploy quick applications on the cloud (without needing a server or container) using only your web browser. They allow you to scale from zero to a very large number of users We will now take a look at the steps involved in creating a Cloud Function to implement a simple Cloud SQL application in Java:

1. Go to the **Cloud Functions** page by searching for it in the **Console** search bar.

2. Click on **Create a function**. Enable the required APIs as prompted by clicking the **ENABLE** button to get started, as shown in the following figure:

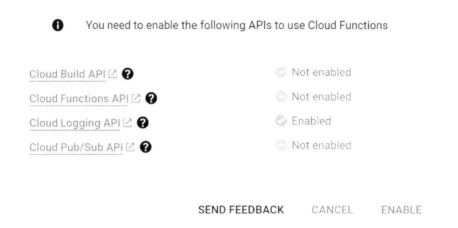

Figure 4.14 – Enabling the APIs

You should be able to configure your Cloud Functions once the APIs are enabled.

3.   Select **2nd gen** for **Environment**, as shown in the following figure:

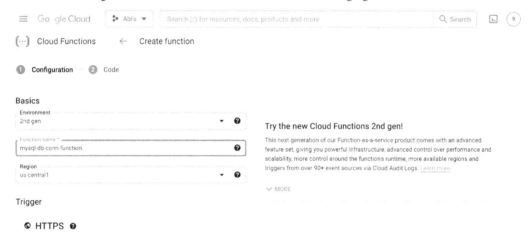

Figure 4.15 – The 2nd gen environment selected with a function name and region populated

4.   In the function name, enter `mysql-db-conn-function`, select **unauthenticated invocation** for demo purposes (the recommendation is to use authentication for real-world applications), and click **Next**.

5.   You will land on a page that lets you select **Runtime** on the left pane. We will select **Java 11**.

6.   In the source code menu, choose **Inline Editor**.

7. In the `pom.xml` file, include the following dependencies inside the `<dependencies></dependencies>` section to ensure you have the necessary package to connect to the Cloud SQL database we created:

```xml
<dependency>
    <groupId>com.google.cloud.sql</groupId>
    <artifactId>mysql-socket-factory-connector-j-8</artifactId>
    <version>1.13.1</version>
</dependency>

<dependency>
    <groupId>mysql</groupId>
    <artifactId>mysql-connector-java</artifactId>
    <version>8.0.29</version>
</dependency>

<dependency>
    <groupId>com.zaxxer</groupId>
    <artifactId>HikariCP</artifactId>
    <version>5.0.1</version>
</dependency>
```

8. You will see some placeholder code similar to the one you see in the `HelloHttpFunction.java` function in the following figure:

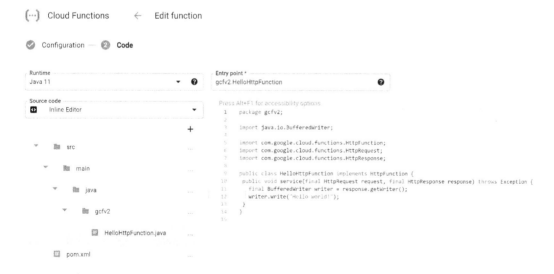

Figure 4.16 – The Edit function page with the default code populated in HelloHttpFunction.java

9. Add the following additional import statements to the code:

```
import java.io.BufferedWriter;
import com.google.cloud.functions.HttpFunction;
import com.google.cloud.functions.HttpRequest;
import com.google.cloud.functions.HttpResponse;
import com.google.common.collect.ImmutableList;
import com.zaxxer.hikari.HikariConfig;
import com.zaxxer.hikari.HikariDataSource;
import java.sql.*;
import java.util.ArrayList;
import java.util.List;
import java.util.Properties;
import java.util.concurrent.TimeUnit;
import java.sql.PreparedStatement;
import java.sql.ResultSet;
import java.sql.Connection;
import java.sql.SQLException;
```

10. Include a `createConnection` method invocation statement at the beginning of the code. There should already be a placeholder code in the `HelloHttpFunction.java` file. Just replace the code in that file with this code. This snippet represents the `HelloHttpFunction` class we are creating, and it implements the `HttpFunction` interface. Also, remember that saving credentials in environment variables is convenient, but not secure—consider a more secure solution, such as the one found at `https://cloud.google.com/kms/`, to help keep your secrets safe:

```
/* Class HelloHttpFunction starts here and it implements the
interface HttpFunction*/
public class HelloHttpFunction implements HttpFunction {
/* Declare the static and final variables for instance
connection name, user, password, and database and replace them
with your values.
You can get the instance connection name from the Cloud SQL
Instance Overview page.
*/
  private static final String INSTANCE_CONNECTION_NAME ="<<your_
project_name>>:<<region>>:<<instance-name>>";
  private static final String DB_USER = "root";
  private static final String DB_PASS = "<<your_password>>";
  private static final String DB_NAME = "test_db";
  private static final String INSTANCE_UNIX_SOCKET = null;
  private HikariDataSource connectionPool;
```

```
/* The service method starts here and it has 2 arguments -
HttpRequest object and HttpResponse object
It establishes the connection to the Cloud SQL MySQL instance
*/
  public void service(final HttpRequest request, final
HttpResponse response) throws Exception {
    final BufferedWriter writer = response.getWriter();
    String jdbcURL = String.format("jdbc:mysql:///%s", DB_NAME);
    Properties connProps = new Properties();
    connProps.setProperty("user", DB_USER);
    connProps.setProperty("password", DB_PASS);
    connProps.setProperty("socketFactory", "com.google.cloud.
sql.mysql.SocketFactory");
    connProps.setProperty("cloudSqlInstance", INSTANCE_
CONNECTION_NAME);

    /* Initialize connection pool */
    HikariConfig config = new HikariConfig();
    config.setJdbcUrl(jdbcURL);
    config.setDataSourceProperties(connProps);
    config.setConnectionTimeout(10000); // 10s

    this.connectionPool = new HikariDataSource(config);
    String result = "";

/* This part of the function invokes the DB connection.
It stores the SELECT query in a variable called query and
invokes the Prepared Statement.
The result is stored in a variable and returned to the
BufferedWriter object.
*/

    try (Connection conn = connectionPool.getConnection()) {
      // PreparedStatements can be more efficient and project
against injections.
      String query =  "select string_column from test_db.test_
table where index_column = 1;";
      PreparedStatement pStmt = conn.prepareStatement(query);
      ResultSet rs = pStmt.executeQuery();
       while(rs.next()) {
            //Set values from result
            result = rs.getString("string_column");
             }
```

```
            } catch (SQLException ex) {
                throw new RuntimeException( "Unable to process. Run
    Time Error in Select.", ex);
            }

        writer.write("Hello! " + result);
        }
    }
}
```

This class is designed to connect to the MySQL database and perform a **Select Query** action in the Cloud SQL database.

11. Once you have successfully completed the aforementioned steps, it is time to deploy the application. Hit **Deploy** at the bottom of the screen to submit the application to the cloud.

12. If there are errors, you will see them on the top of the screen or in the logs section.

13. If not, you will see your application running on the cloud, as shown in the following figure:

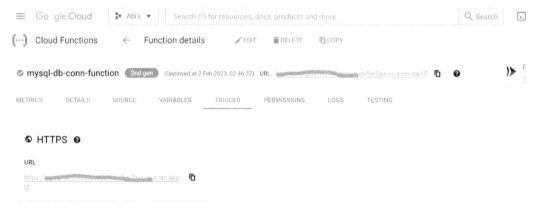

Figure 4.17 – The deployed URL of the Cloud Function

14. Click the HTTPS link in the **URL** section of the deployed Cloud Function. If it shows an error with permission, navigate to the **PERMISSIONS** tab, click **GRANT ACCESS**, and make sure you add the necessary users or `allUsers` and grant them the **Cloud Functions Invoker** role, as shown in the following screenshot:

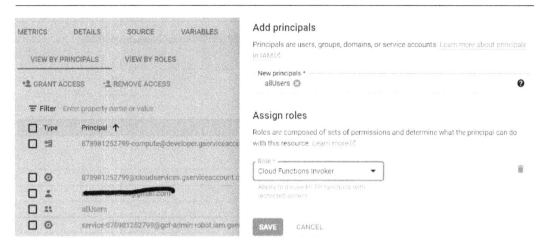

Figure 4.18 – Configuring permissions for the deployed Cloud Function

15. That is not all. Since we are using Cloud Functions 2nd Gen, we have to also check authentication for the underlying Cloud Run service as well. Navigate to the underlying Cloud Run service by clicking the service name link in the right corner of the Cloud Functions page (underlined in black in the following screenshot):

Figure 4.19 – Navigating to the Cloud Run service

In the Cloud Run service page that opens, navigate to the **SECURITY** tab and select **Allow unauthenticated invocations** for this demo (or **Require authentication** per your application's requirements), as shown here:

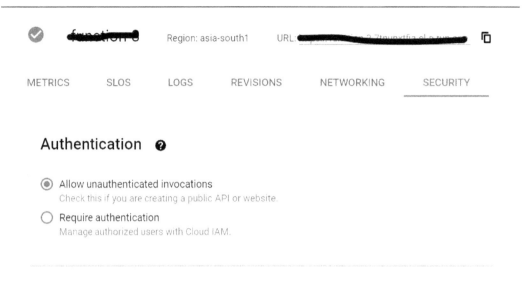

Figure 4.20 – Authenticating the Cloud Run service

Now you can return to the Cloud Functions page and click the URL on the **TRIGGER** tab of the Cloud Function you deployed in *step 13*. The result of the Cloud Function trigger on the browser looks like this:

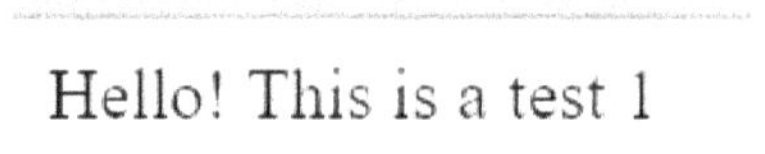

Hello! This is a test 1

Figure 4.21 – The output of the Cloud Function trigger

That's it! We have successfully set up a database and created a small Cloud Functions application that is running on the cloud.

So far, you have learned about the fully managed relational Google Cloud database Cloud SQL, instance setup and configuration, database creation, basic functional queries and DDL statements, and a programmatic approach to connect and access data on your Cloud SQL instance. The program we created to connect to the database is in Java and can be deployed serverlessly with Cloud Functions. In the next section, we will look at some operational aspects of this database.

Operational aspects of cloud relational databases

Apart from the key features and setup details we discussed so far, there are some key operational considerations that every organization or startup needs to assess before starting their database design journey. We will look at only a few key operational considerations and how Cloud SQL supports these aspects.

Migration

Cloud SQL's Database Migration Service comes in handy from the Google Cloud perspective; it simplifies migrations on-premise or from other cloud providers to Google Cloud SQL. Its key features are that it is very simple, has minimal downtime migration, and is fully serverless to set up without any operational burden.

Monitoring

We can monitor Cloud SQL instances from the Cloud Monitoring dashboard to cover metrics such as CPU utilization, active connections, storage usage, memory usage, read and write operations, ingress and egress bytes, queries, questions, and so much more.

Query Insights

Beyond monitoring instances, Cloud SQL offers the Query Insights tool, which allows us to derive insights from queries' performance problems and diagnostic information and helps us identify the root cause of the performance problems. We can monitor performance at the application component level identified by the model, view, and controller layers of the application. This makes it the first of its kind for top-down (app to query) and bottom-up (query to app layers) insights into database query performance.

Security

The most important operational aspect of any database application is security considerations. Along with this comes encryption requirements (both at rest and in transit), privacy, regulatory requirements, firewalls, access control, and so on. Cloud SQL data is encrypted when on Google's internal networks and when stored in database tables, temporary files, and backups. It supports private connectivity with a **virtual private cloud** (**VPC**), and every Cloud SQL instance includes a network firewall, allowing you to control public network access. You can also configure where your data is stored to comply with data residency requirements. Cloud SQL is compliant with SSAE 16, ISO 27001, and PCI DSS and supports **Health Insurance Portability and Accountability Act** (**HIPAA**) compliance.

There are many operational considerations to look into while designing your database, such as high availability, change data capture, and replication, that will ensure your database is fully equipped to support your application and business needs.

Summary

In this chapter, we have designed a structured database via hands-on learning by creating and configuring a fully managed cloud relational database. We discussed the essential features of a fully managed RDBMS: Google Cloud's Cloud SQL. We covered the setup and configuration of Cloud SQL, created a database and objects, performed database operations on it programmatically, and assessed design considerations and operational highlights such as migration, monitoring, query insights, and security when working with Cloud SQL. We also created a one-page application to access Cloud SQL with a Java Cloud Function as an example.

In the upcoming chapters, we will move on to other formats of data, hands-on applications, and their operational aspects.

5

Designing an Analytical Data Warehouse

In the previous chapter, we discussed hands-on database design for structured data and design considerations. Then, we learned how to set up, configure, and create database objects, connect to the database, and access data programmatically. In this chapter, we will move on to designing for analytical data and start hands-on learning with a fully managed cloud data warehouse. In doing so, you will learn how to set up and configure databases, create datasets and objects, and query and perform sample analytics on data.

In this chapter, we'll cover the following topics:

- Understanding how data warehouses are different from databases
- The significance of ETL in data warehouses
- BigQuery hands-on
- Summary of operational aspects and design considerations

Understanding how data warehouses are different from databases

Data warehousing is the process of storing and managing data from multiple sources in a centralized location. This makes it easier to analyze the data and gain insights that can be used to improve business operations. Data warehouse applications are designed to support mainly, but not limited to, **online analytical processing (OLAP)** data models, which are centered around the dimensions of data that the business organizes. Such modes of data warehouse tend to facilitate data aggregation for summary, drilling down into details, slicing and dicing across dimensions, querying for analysis, and making business decisions.

In contrast to the database applications that support transactional models (OLTP), which are intended for a specific functional application or product of the business, data warehouses support models that are meant for the entire business and organization, not just for a specific group of users (access control for users and groups can be provisioned) or functionality; they are meant to store current and historical records of transactions and other dependent data from varied sources as applicable.

Data warehousing can be used by businesses of all sizes and in all industries. It is a powerful tool that can be used to improve **business intelligence** (**BI**), make better decisions, and gain a competitive advantage. Here are some real-world examples of data warehouse use cases across various industries:

- **Retail analytics**: A retail company uses a data warehouse to consolidate data from various sources, including sales transactions, online customer interactions, and inventory levels. They analyze this data to optimize inventory management, predict demand, and personalize marketing campaigns based on customer behavior.

- **Healthcare management**: A healthcare provider uses a data warehouse to store patient records, medical histories, and billing information. They apply data analytics to identify trends in patient outcomes, streamline administrative processes, and enhance patient care by predicting disease outbreaks and optimizing resource allocation.

- **Financial services**: A financial institution leverages a data warehouse to integrate data from multiple branches, customer accounts, and transaction records. They utilize this data to detect fraudulent activities, assess credit risk, and provide personalized financial recommendations to clients.

- **Manufacturing quality control**: A manufacturing company employs a data warehouse to collect data from sensors on the factory floor, such as machine performance, defect rates, and production output. This data helps them identify quality issues, improve production efficiency, and reduce downtime by predicting equipment maintenance needs.

- **E-commerce recommendations**: An e-commerce platform utilizes a data warehouse to store customer behavior data, purchase history, and product catalog information. They apply machine learning algorithms to make real-time product recommendations, leading to increased sales and improved customer satisfaction.

- **Supply chain optimization**: A logistics company centralizes data related to shipments, transportation routes, and warehouse inventory in a data warehouse. They use this data to optimize delivery routes, reduce shipping costs, and minimize inventory holding costs while ensuring products reach customers on time.

- **Energy consumption analysis**: An energy utility provider aggregates data from smart meters, weather forecasts, and customer demographics in a data warehouse. They use predictive analytics to anticipate energy demand, optimize energy distribution, and offer customers personalized energy-saving suggestions.

- **Media and entertainment**: A streaming platform stores user interaction data, content libraries, and add performance metrics in a data warehouse. They employ this data to improve content recommendations, target advertising more effectively, and measure viewer engagement.

- **Government and public policy**: A government agency compiles data from various departments, including healthcare, education, and transportation, in a data warehouse. They use this data to inform policy decisions, allocate resources efficiently, and measure the impact of government programs on citizens' well-being.

- **Customer experience enhancement**: A customer-centric business aggregates data from customer support interactions, feedback surveys, and social media sentiment analysis in a data warehouse. They leverage this data to identify pain points in the customer journey, improve customer service, and enhance overall customer experience.

These examples demonstrate the versatility of data warehouses in helping organizations make informed decisions, optimize operations, and gain competitive advantages across diverse industries.

Let's quickly take a look at some of the core characteristics and attributes of data warehouses:

- Data warehouses are mostly designed for analytics, analysis, reporting, and BI purposes

- Data warehouses serve the whole business and organization in making decisions

- Data warehouses provide a bigger picture as well as a detailed outlook of transactions and dependencies, both current and historical

- Since they are mostly analytical, they are read-intensive

- Data from multiple sources and formats are integrated as part of the loading process for data warehouses

The following table summarizes a few of the core differences in characteristics of a purely transactional versus analytical database system:

Characteristic	Transactional database	Analytical database
Purpose	Record and process transactions	Analyze data for insights
Data structure	Normalized	Denormalized
Data volume	High	Low
Query complexity	Low	High
Update frequency	High	Low

Figure 5.1 – Differences between a transactional and analytical database

To summarize, transactional databases are used to support business-critical applications such as order processing, inventory management, and **customer relationship management** (**CRM**). Analytical databases are used to support data warehousing and BI applications. These applications help businesses understand their data and make better decisions.

Since these analytical applications are used by businesses to handle large data from different sources, we would need a process to move data from one system to another so that businesses can integrate data from different sources into a single data warehouse, where it can be analyzed to gain insights. This process is called ETL, which is exactly what we are going to discuss in the next section.

Significance of ETL in data warehouse

ETL is a process in data warehousing that represents **extract, transform, and load**. This process involves extracting data from multiple sources, transforming and performing computations, cleansing for data quality, and loading the data into a target system. ETL is important for data warehouses to collect, read, process, transform, migrate, and analyze data from several disparate sources into one target database or warehouse. ETL eliminates silos in sources and integrates data for easy access and BI.

The ETL process typically consists of the following steps:

- **Extract/ingest**: Data is extracted from the source systems. This can be done using a variety of methods, such as database queries, file transfers, or APIs.

- **Transform**: The data is transformed into a format that is compatible with the target system. This may involve cleaning the data, converting data types, or merging data from multiple sources.

- **Load**: The data is loaded into the target system. This can be done using a variety of methods, such as database inserts, file transfers, batch processes, or APIs.

ETL is important to analytical systems because it allows businesses to do the following:

- **Integrate data from different sources**: Businesses often have data stored in different systems, such as CRM systems, **enterprise resource planning** (**ERP**) systems, and **point-of-sale** (**POS**) systems. ETL allows businesses to integrate data from these different systems into a single data warehouse, where it can be analyzed to gain insights.

- **Cleanse and transform data**: Data from different sources may be in different formats and may contain errors. ETL allows businesses to cleanse and transform the data into a format that is compatible with the target system and that is suitable for analysis.

- **Load data into the target system**: ETL allows businesses to load data into the target system in a way that is efficient and reliable.

ETL is a critical component of many analytical systems. By integrating data from different sources, cleansing and transforming data, and loading data into the target system, ETL allows businesses to gain insights from their data that would not be possible otherwise. Depending on the nature of the data, requirements, and limitations for your business, you can choose the type of ETL tools and services, including custom on-demand development, batch processing, real-time, and cloud service options.

Some of the cloud offerings that can be used to extract, transform, and load data are as follows:

- **Cloud Dataflow**: This is a fully managed service for stream and batch data processing. Dataflow can be used to extract data from a variety of sources, including databases, messaging systems, and files, as well as to transform data in a variety of ways, such as cleaning data, converting data types, and merging data from multiple sources.

- **Cloud Data Fusion**: This is a fully managed, cloud-native, enterprise data integration service that helps you build and manage ETL data pipelines. Data Fusion can be used to extract and transform data from a variety of sources, including databases, SaaS applications, and cloud storage services.

- **Cloud Data Catalog**: This is a fully managed data discovery and metadata management service. Data Catalog can be used to discover and understand data sources, which can make the extraction process easier.

- **Cloud Dataproc**: This is a fully managed and highly scalable service for running Apache Hadoop, Apache Spark, Apache Flink, Presto, and several open source tools and frameworks. Dataproc can be used to transform data using a variety of big data processing tools.

- **BigQuery**: This is a fully managed, petabyte-scale analytics data warehouse. BigQuery can be used to load data from a variety of sources, including databases, files, and other cloud storage services. BigQuery can also be used to perform machine learning and generative AI analytics on analytics data and can store and process structured, semi-structured, and unstructured data.

- **Cloud Storage**: This is a durable and highly available object storage service. Cloud Storage can be used as a staging area for data before it is loaded into the target system.

Google Cloud offers a variety of services that can be used to implement an ETL pipeline. The specific services that you use will depend on your specific needs.

To summarize, ETL is a fundamental process in the analytical application life cycle that ensures data is collected, cleaned, transformed, and loaded into a suitable repository, making it ready for analysis and reporting. It plays a crucial role in turning raw data into valuable insights for businesses. Of all the services and tools that are available, we will be looking at the role of BigQuery in the ETL process of handling analytical data workloads with relational data structure in the upcoming sections.

Learning about BigQuery

BigQuery is a fully managed, completely serverless (no need to think about the underlying infrastructure), cost-effective, petabyte-scale enterprise data warehouse with built-in machine learning and BI analytics that works across clouds and sources and scales with your data. It is an important service for the transform (process, analyze) stage in the life cycle of your data.

An entire book can be dedicated to BigQuery and it still wouldn't be sufficient to cover everything that BigQuery has to offer for your data and businesses in its fullest sense. We will take a look at the key features in the next section and try some of these hands-on in this chapter.

Features of BigQuery

In this section, I have tried to address the features that database practitioners and developers associate with the most:

- With BigQuery, you can unify structured, unstructured, and semi-structured data and perform queries on them together. This means you can also use this unification to derive machine learning insights with attributes of varied structures and types.

- BigQuery has built-in machine learning capabilities that allow analysts and businesses to create models on planet-scale structured, semi-structured, and unstructured data using simple SQL queries in seconds.

- BigQuery Studio provides a single, unified interface for all data practitioners for taking data to AI, including ingestion, exploration, visualization, and machine learning model creation all in simplified workflows. It also supports access to Vertex AI's foundation models for text generation and processing tasks.

- BigQuery has an AI collaborator named Duet AI integrated into it so that it can provide contextual code assistance for writing SQL and Python and generate auto-suggestions for functions, code blocks, and fixes. You can also use natural language to get help using chat assistance.

- BigQuery supports data movement and analysis across multi-cloud and hybrid data stores and shares the results in a single pane of glass view.

- BigQuery has real-time analytics capabilities with query acceleration that makes querying on streaming data fast and robust.

- BigQuery's Connected Sheets allows users to analyze billions of rows without requiring SQLs. Users can also apply visualization to derive insights from its data.

- BigQuery provides low latency data synchronization across varied databases and storage with real-time change data capture and up-to-date replication for real-time analytics.

- BigQuery allows you to optimize query performance costs with materialized views for quickly getting answers to common business questions.

- BigQuery integrates with Google's privacy and security services to provide fine-grained governance controls, and data is encrypted at rest and in transit.

- My personal favorite is that BigQuery provides access to a powerful data repository with all the public datasets from different industries with free storage and up to 1 TB of data querying per month at no cost, at the time of writing this book.

For a list of detailed features, refer to the Google Cloud documentation for BigQuery: `https://cloud.google.com/bigquery`.

In the remainder of this section, we will learn how to set up and manage an analytical data warehouse on Google Cloud with BigQuery and take a sneak peek at some easy analytics.

> **Note**
>
> Please be advised that certain features and services described in the below sections may have undergone modifications since the time of drafting. The screenshots may look different from what you see in the book. APIs and versions may have been updated by the time you are reading this. As such, kindly exercise flexibility and adapt your steps accordingly.
>
> Additionally, some services may incur charges if they are outside the free tier (if applicable). Therefore, it is recommended to be aware of the services you are enabling and to delete or deactivate services and instances that are no longer required for learning or demonstration purposes.

Setting up and configuring a fully managed data warehouse with BigQuery

If you are new to Google Cloud, go to Google Cloud Console (`https://console.cloud.google.com/`), select your organization, and create a new Google Cloud project with billing enabled. You can follow the instructions here: `https://cloud.google.com/resource-manager/docs/creating-managing-projects`.

You can use your free credits if you have it or BigQuery Sandbox (`https://cloud.google.com/bigquery/docs/sandbox`) to use BigQuery for free.

All the steps mentioned here can be completed with Command Shell commands, Google Cloud Console, or programmatically. While we will use the BigQuery console option here, if you would like to experiment with the other two options, feel free to do so. The following are links to resources for the Command Shell method, Client library, and BigQuery API:

- `https://cloud.google.com/bigquery/docs/bq-command-line-tool`
- `https://cloud.google.com/bigquery/docs/reference/libraries`
- `https://cloud.google.com/bigquery/docs/reference/rest/v2/datasets`

Enabling BigQuery from the console

To enable BigQuery, follow these steps:

1. Go to Google Cloud Console and, in the search bar, search for `BigQuery`. If it is not already enabled, you will be prompted to enable the BigQuery API for your project.

2. Continue following the prompt. Alternatively, you can go to the BigQuery console: `https://console.cloud.google.com/bigquery`. The following screenshot shows the BigQuery console:

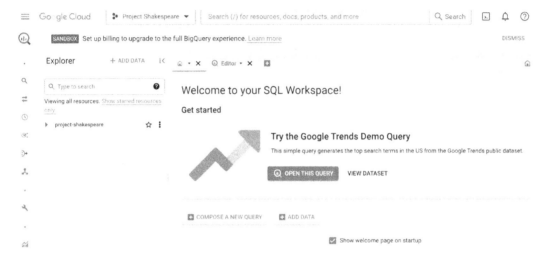

Figure 5.2 – The BigQuery console

As you can see, the BigQuery console has the **Explorer** pane on the left and the query editor on the right.

3. Now that you have successfully landed on the console, you can start creating the dataset. The steps provided here can be performed in many ways – from the BigQuery console or programmatically using APIs or using the `bq` command-line commands.

4. `bq` is a Python-based command-line tool that can be used for interacting with BigQuery data. The commands can be entered in Cloud Shell. To start, click **Activate Cloud Shell from Google Cloud Console** in the top-right corner, as shown here:

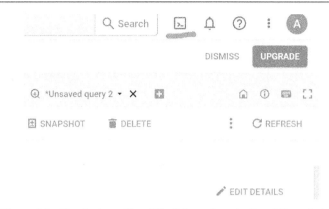

Figure 5.3 – The Activate Cloud Shell from Google Cloud Console icon

Once activated, you can either use bq commands from the Cloud Shell terminal or the BigQuery console to complete the remaining steps.

Alternatively, you can try out the steps programmatically using client libraries or APIs. I have chosen to use the BigQuery console for the rest of the steps.

Creating a BigQuery dataset

A **BigQuery dataset** is a top-level container that lives within a specific project. This can be compared to a schema in traditional relational databases and data warehouses as it organizes and manages the tables, views, and other objects of that schema.

Remember that a dataset is created in a specific location. The location of a dataset cannot be changed after creation; you can only copy or recreate the dataset manually to a different location. Dataset names should be unique within a project.

The following screenshot shows how to create a dataset:

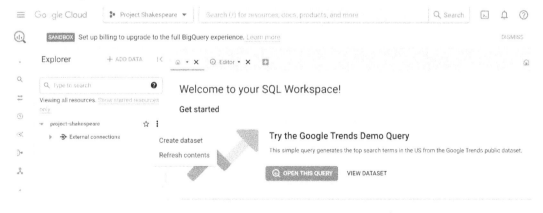

Figure 5.4 – BigQuery dataset creation

As you can see, when you click the three dots next to the project name and the star, you can view the list of actions you can take on the project – **Create dataset** and **Refresh contents**.

Select the **Create dataset** option. This will open the **Create dataset** configuration page, as shown here:

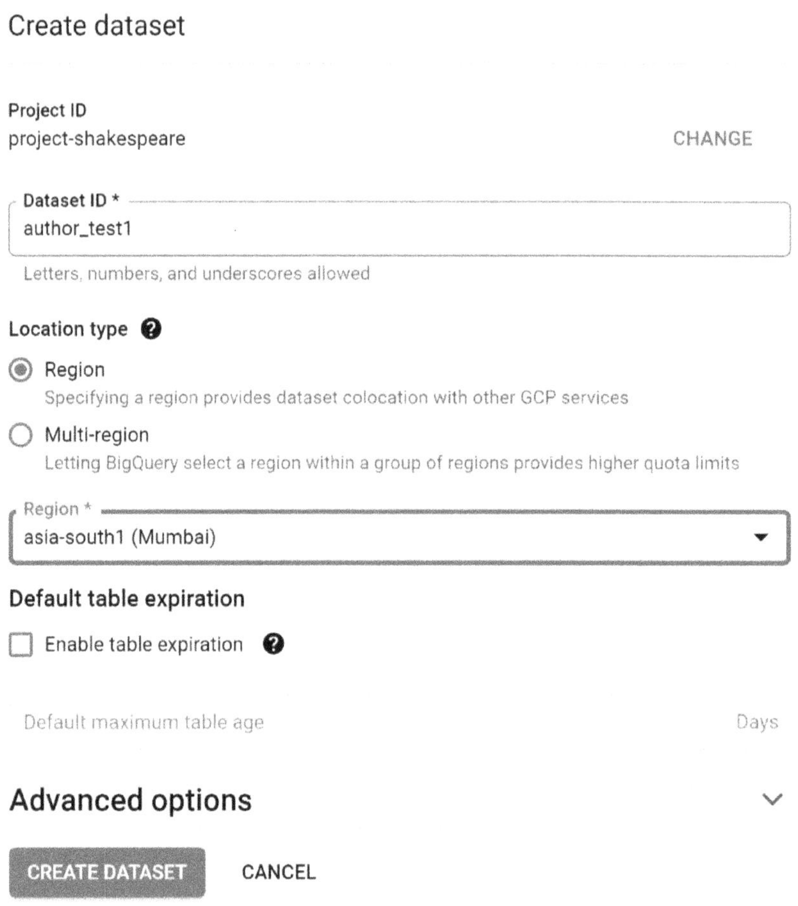

Create dataset

Project ID
project-shakespeare   CHANGE

Dataset ID *
author_test1

Letters, numbers, and underscores allowed

Location type ❓

◉ Region
    Specifying a region provides dataset colocation with other GCP services

◯ Multi-region
    Letting BigQuery select a region within a group of regions provides higher quota limits

Region *
asia-south1 (Mumbai)   ▼

Default table expiration

☐ Enable table expiration ❓

Default maximum table age   Days

Advanced options   ⌄

CREATE DATASET   CANCEL

Figure 5.5 – Create dataset

On the **Create dataset** configuration page, as seen in the preceding screenshot, you have **Dataset ID**, **Location type**, and other configuration options. Make sure the location and other choices you make here are a result of the design considerations and security requirements for your data and business requirements. In this case, this is a test entry.

As you might have noticed, we have created a dataset explicitly for our application's needs. Imagine a scenario where you don't have data to begin with, but want to leverage openly available data. You could use BigQuery's public datasets for that instead of creating a dataset that will contain your data.

Using an existing public dataset

Public datasets are hosted and stored in BigQuery. These are available for access from your projects and can be integrated into applications. Google takes care of storing these datasets and you only pay for the queries you perform on it.

You can access public datasets from Google Cloud Console by following these steps:

1. In BigQuery's **Explorer** pane, in the **Type to search** field, enter `bigquery-public-data` to see if the dataset is starred. It won't be unless you have already starred `bigquery-public-data` to **Explorer**. The following screenshot shows `bigquery-public-data` entered in the **Type to search** field:

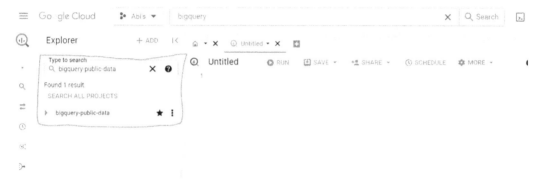

Figure 5.6 – BigQuery public dataset search

As you can see, I have already starred (saved it as a favorite) the BigQuery public data project.

2. If it is not present, search for a specific dataset or table contained in the public dataset by typing in the **Type to Search** field. As an example, type `covid19_open_data` and click **SEARCH ALL PROJECTS**.

3. In the **Explorer** pane, you will see **bigquery-public-data**. Click the star icon next to it.

4. Enter `bigquery-public-data` in the **Type to Search** field again and once it appears, **Expand** this project.

5. Once you have expanded it, you can query the dataset from the Query Editor by clicking **Compose new query**, as shown here:

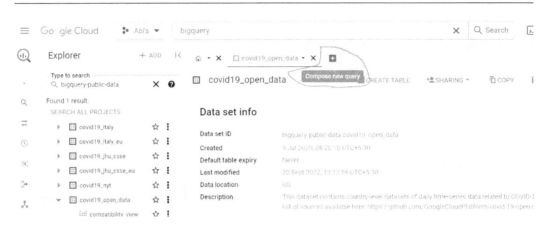

Figure 5.7 – Public dataset expanded with Compose new query highlighted

As you can see, the **covid19_open_data** public dataset has been expanded. I have also highlighted the **Compose new query** icon for your reference.

Once the dataset is ready, be it public or your own new dataset, you should be able to create other objects and dependencies that are required for your application. In the next few sections, we will create objects on the custom dataset we created previously and play with the data using BigQuery queries.

Creating a table in the dataset

Tables contain records (rows) and fields (columns). There are three types of tables in BigQuery:

- Standard
- External
- Views

Standard tables are for structured data containing rows and columns. **External tables** are stored outside of BigQuery and the data can be structured or unstructured. **Views** are logical tables that are run only when the queries are executed. Materialized views, however, have a pre-computed cache of results of the view query.

To create a table, you can either run the respective *DDL* statement or do so from the BigQuery console's **Explorer** pane:

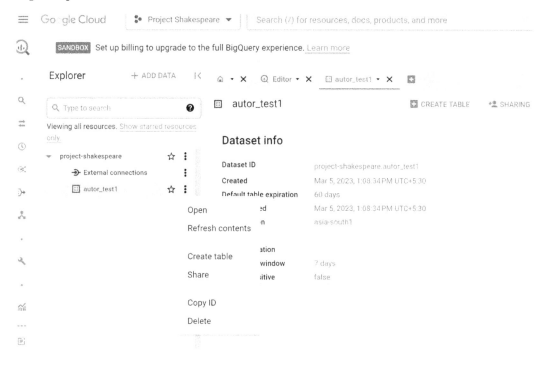

Figure 5.8 – The Create table option listed in the dataset

Click **Create table**, you should see the **Create table** dialogue appear. Enter the necessary details, as shown here:

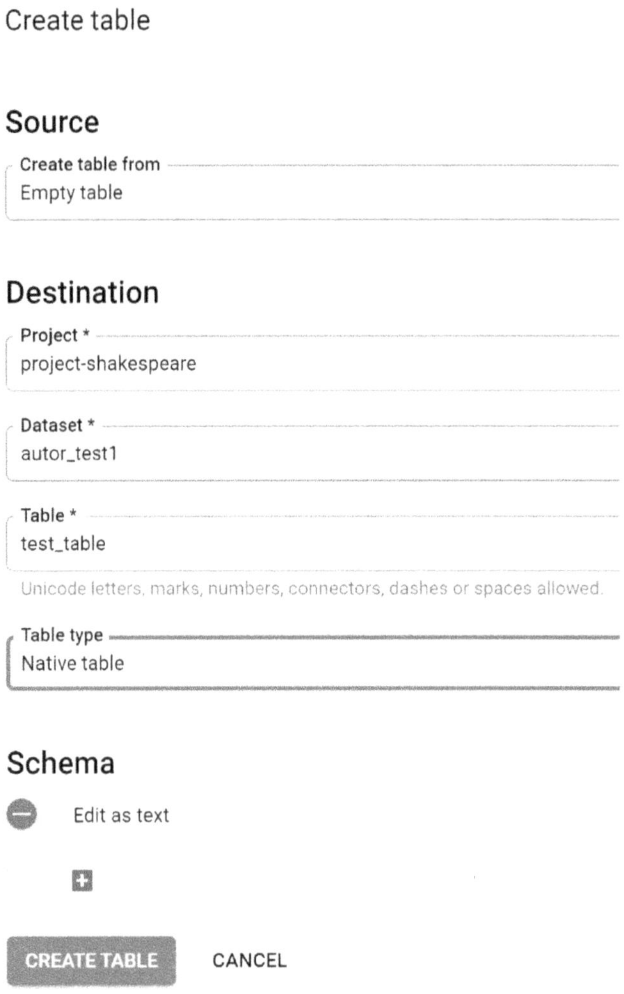

Create table

Source

Create table from
Empty table

Destination

Project *
project-shakespeare

Dataset *
autor_test1

Table *
test_table

Unicode letters, marks, numbers, connectors, dashes or spaces allowed.

Table type
Native table

Schema

⊖   Edit as text

➕

CREATE TABLE   CANCEL

Figure 5.9 – The Create table configuration page

Here, you can define the table schema – you can define columns, data types, and constraints by clicking on the + sign in the **Edit Schema** section, as shown here:

Edit Schema

Current schema

ADD POLICY TAG

	Field name	Type	Mode	Collation	Default Value ❓	Policy Tags ❓	Description
☐	NAME	STRING(50)	NULLABLE		Default Value		Description
☐	TITLE	STRING(25)	NULLABLE		Default Value		Description
☐	ID	INTEGER	NULLABLE		Default Value		Description
☐	DEPARTMENT	STRING(25)	NULLABLE		Default Value		Description

New fields

➖ Edit as text

➕

SAVE   CLOSE

Figure 5.10 – The Edit Schema page

As shown in the preceding screenshot, you enter the field names and the relevant details and click **Save**.

Now that the table has been created, let's insert data into it.

Inserting values in BigQuery tables

You can load data into BigQuery tables using *DML* statements, programmatically with the client libraries/APIs, or using the bq Cloud Shell command.

In this section, for a change, we'll use the bq command to load data into the BigQuery table we just created – that is, test_table. We can execute bq commands from the Cloud Shell terminal. Create a CSV file containing sample data for the id (numeric), name (string), title (string), and department (string) fields and upload it to the folder from where you are executing the following command in Cloud Shell. Alternatively, you can download any sample CSV file and match the structure (that is, the field names and data type) using the BigQuery load command:

```
bq load --source_format=CSV --skip_leading_rows=1 autor_test1.test_
table \
./author_test.csv \
id:numeric,name:string,title:string,department:string
```

This command will load the data you have in the author_test.csv file into the test_table table we just created. Please note that the command assumes you have the CSV file in the directory from which you are running this command in the terminal.

Alternatively, you can use the traditional `INSERT` DML statement to insert rows into the table. You can also insert data programmatically into BigQuery tables using the BigQuery API. I provided the reference links to these other options at the very beginning of this section, *Setting up and configuring a fully managed data warehouse with BigQuery*. Try the other options out as a hands-on assignment at the end of this chapter.

In this subsection, we inserted data from a CSV file into our BigQuery table. There are multiple ways to load data into BigQuery, including BigQuery's data transfer service, batch load, using the Storage API to read and write data, and more. While we won't be discussing all these options in this book, we can talk about one of the options – streaming data into BigQuery – at a high level in the next sub-section.

Streaming data into BigQuery

It is possible to stream data into BigQuery. Here, you send small batches of continuous data in real time. This means the real-time data is immediately available for querying and analytics or other purposes for your application. To stream data into BigQuery, you can use the *Storage Write API* programmatically in your application. You have to consider whether your application needs *at least once* streaming of a record or *exactly once* streaming, depending on which you will either use the Default or the Committed type for your implementation, respectively. This could be a major design decision based on the requirement for your application's analytics. For instance, the *at least once* streaming of a record indicates that your application can accept duplicates that appear in the destination table in BigQuery. You can use the *Default* stream for this. The *exactly once* streaming of a record indicates that your application requires the record to be streamed exactly once and you can use the Committed stream type.

To learn more about different ways of loading data into BigQuery, refer to the necessary documentation: `https://cloud.google.com/bigquery/docs/loading-data`. You must assess the type of ingestion that would work best for your business needs at design time itself.

Now that we have created a dataset, created a table, and loaded data into that table, we will perform analytics on the data.

Performing simple analytics

To perform simple analytics, we'll use a BigQuery public dataset called *covid19_open_data*. Follow these steps:

1. Search for `covid19_open_data` in the **Type to search** field in the **Explorer** pane and star **bigquery-public-data.**

2. Expand **bigquery-public-data** and search for `covid19_open_data` again.

3. Click on the three dots next to the **covid19_open_data** table and click **Open.**

4. Click the **SCHEMA** tab to view the columns and details of the table.

5. Click the **QUERY** option at the top and select **open in new tab**.

> **Note**
> If you are running this as a sample experiment, make sure you are using the sandbox environment by checking for the **SANDBOX** tag at the top left of your BigQuery console.

Execute the following query to view a portion of the table's contents:

```
SELECT country_name, new_confirmed, date, cumulative_confirmed,
population FROM `bigquery-public-data.covid19_open_data.covid19_open_
data` LIMIT 10
```

This is a basic `SELECT` statement for viewing the fields we are going to use to create the analytical query. The following screenshot shows the results for this query:

Row	country_name	new_confirmed	date	cumulative_confirme	population
1	Andorra	114	2021-01-19	9308	77265
2	Andorra	0	2020-06-09	852	77265
3	Andorra	49	2021-03-24	11687	77265
4	Andorra	1	2020-06-17	855	77265
5	Andorra	57	2020-04-04	523	77265
6	Andorra	14	2021-09-05	15069	77265
7	Andorra	9	2021-06-22	13873	77265
8	Andorra	3	2021-06-17	13842	77265
9	United Arab Emirates	626	2020-09-27	92095	9890400
10	United Arab Emirates	1070	2021-08-19	707236	9890400

Figure 5.11 – Select query results

Let's try to summarize and display the top five countries with the most confirmed COVID-19 numbers:

```
SELECT country_name, MAX(cumulative_confirmed) AS TOTAL_CONFIRMED_
COVID19
FROM `bigquery-public-data.covid19_open_data.covid19_open_data`
WHERE cumulative_confirmed > 0
GROUP BY country_name
ORDER BY MAX(cumulative_confirmed) DESC
LIMIT 5;
```

Once you execute this query, you will see the following output:

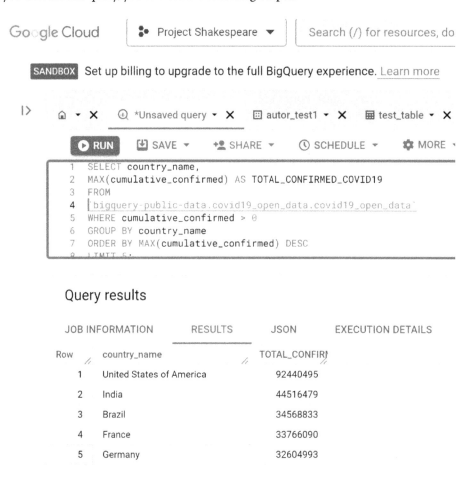

Figure 5.12 – Basic analytics query with results

The same query can be executed in several ways – running the query from the BigQuery console (which is what we have done), using the bq query command, or using the *BigQuery API* to run it programmatically for your application. As in the previous section, I have left the other two options as a challenge for you to implement.

Now that we have discussed the data warehouse setup and how to run basic analytics, we are ready to end this chapter with a quick summary of the operational and design aspects of this process.

Summary of operational aspects and design considerations

When you are evaluating a cloud data warehouse or analytical storage for your application, make sure you design for the following key operational aspects:

- **Data warehouse migration**: Ensure the choice and configuration for your data warehouse supports easy migration of your data to the cloud data warehouse in case your application requires it.

- **Transferring data**: Consider the need to efficiently move and synchronize data between different systems and platforms. The format and way you ingest data into BigQuery is an important aspect, as we discussed earlier.

- **Data governance and security options**: Make sure your choice of data warehouse or analytics system allows you to implement robust security measures and governance practices to protect your data.

- **Real-time and predictive analytics**: While designing an analytics solution, also consider enabling real-time data processing and predictive analytics for actionable insights with your data. Prescriptive analytics is the order of the day.

- **Logging data for analytics**: One very flexible feature a cloud data warehouse system could boast would be that it could collect log data from other services within the cloud platform that your application uses. This would help you analyze log data to monitor and improve overall system performance from within the scope of your warehouse. Consider discussing this as part of your design aspects.

- **Separation of storage and compute functions**: Design for flexibility by separating storage and computational resources.

- **BI features**: Incorporate tools and features for advanced BI and reporting.

- **Fully-managed, serverless**: Opt for a fully managed serverless solution to reduce operational overhead.

- **Support for multi-cloud data analytics**: Ensure compatibility with multiple cloud providers for flexibility, if applicable.

- **Scalable from free-tier coverage to planet-scale usage**: It is very important to design for scaling your data infrastructure from small-scale to global operations as your business grows. Make sure your analytics system is capable of supporting this consideration.

These are critical as your business and application need to meet growing demands. BigQuery supports all of these aspects while working across clouds, scaling with your data, and providing built-in BI, machine learning, and AI.

Summary

In this chapter, we covered the topic of designing for analytical data, understanding the differences between data warehouses and databases, and the importance of data warehouses with real-world use cases. We outlined the core characteristics of data warehouses, highlighting their analytical focus, data integration capabilities, and comprehensive data insights. We also discussed the significance of ETL in a data warehouse application and introduced a few cloud services for ETL, including Cloud Dataflow, Cloud Data Fusion, Cloud Data Catalog, Cloud Dataproc, and BigQuery, all of which aim to provide efficient data movement and transformation capabilities.

We focused on BigQuery, a fully managed serverless data warehouse that provides advanced features such as data unification, built-in machine learning, AI collaboration, real-time analytics, and robust security as it is a powerful tool for handling analytical workloads. We discussed it with a hands-on guide on setting up and configuring a BigQuery data warehouse, including creating datasets, and tables, loading data into tables, hands-on analytics, and SQL snippets. Finally, we covered operational and design aspects.

As a takeaway, I sincerely hope you can try out either one or both of the two other ways to operate on your data in BigQuery – that is `bq` commands/client libraries and APIs. With this, we can conclude our discussion on relational database design for structured data. Next, we will learn how to design for semi-structured, unstructured, and other types of data.

Part 3:
Semi-Structured, Unstructured Data, and NoSQL Design

This part covers what semi-structured data is. You will learn about the difference between SQL and NoSQL. You will also learn all the options available for modeling your semi-structured data application.

This part has the following chapters:

- *Chapter 6*, Designing for *Semi-Structured Data*
- *Chapter 7, Unstructured Data Management*

6

Designing for Semi-Structured Data

So far, we have discussed relational databases and analytics design for structured data. Now, we will look at semi-structured data and design considerations for it by looking at a hands-on example. In this chapter, you will learn about the fundamentals of semi-structured data with examples and real-world use cases, the characteristics of semi-structured data, design considerations, and the components of a document database. We will also explore setting up and configuring a serverless document database (Firestore), creating indexes, and querying your data with APIs.

In this chapter, we'll cover the following topics:

- Semi-structured data
- NoSQL for semi-structured data
- Firestore and its features
- Firestore setup
- Security
- Client libraries and APIs
- Indexing
- Data model considerations
- Easy querying with RunQuery API

Semi-structured data

Semi-structured data does not follow the typical row–column table format or conform to a rigid schema structure; therefore, it cannot fit completely in the relational databases category. However, it is not entirely unstructured either. Semi-structured data is somewhere in between these two categories and is characterized by the following features:

- **Schema flexibility**: It is adaptable to changes and accepts structure in the form of hierarchical data format and keys.

- **Nestedness and hierarchy**: Semi-structured data often has a hierarchical or a nested structure and its data elements are often grouped within other elements, forming a tree-like structure. This results in representations such as **eXtensible Markup Language (XML)** or **JavaScript Object Notation (JSON)**.

- **Without a fixed datatype**: Semi-structured data can have elements of varying data types within the same dataset. For example, a JSON document can contain strings, Booleans, numbers, and nested objects.

- **Sparse data**: This means that semi-structured data need not have all data elements in every instance. This means data storage is used only when there is relevant information.

- **Schema growth/change**: This means that schema can evolve over time with new attributes added over time without breaking existing data, making it easier for scenarios with frequent data and data structure changes.

Semi-structured data is particularly valuable in modern data-driven applications, as it allows for the handling of diverse and evolving data sources. Tools and technologies for managing and querying semi-structured data have gained prominence in data analytics and are crucial in scenarios where data doesn't neatly fit into structured databases but still requires organization and analysis.

Some common examples and sources of semi-structured data include XML data, JSON, email data, files, and web pages. Here is an example of semi-structured data:

```
{
  "order": {
    "order_number": "ORD20231006",
    "order_date": "2023-10-06",
    "customer": {
      "name": "XYZ Enterprises",
      "address": "456 Elm Street",
      "city": "Sometown",
      "state": "NY",
      "postal_code": "54321"
    },
    "items": [
```

```
    {
      "product_id": "P123",
      "description": "Widget A",
      "quantity": 20,
      "unit_price": 10.99
    },
    {
      "product_id": "P456",
      "description": "Gadget B",
      "quantity": 15,
      "unit_price": 19.95
    }
  ],
  "notes": "Please expedite shipping for this order."
  }
}
```

For this JSON example, consider the following:

- `order` is the root object, containing fields such as `order_number`, `order_date`, `customer`, `items`, and `notes`

- `customer` is an embedded object with fields for the customer's name, address, and contact information

- `items` is an array of objects representing the ordered items with fields such as `product_id`, `description`, `quantity`, and `unit_price`

- `notes` contains additional information as a single string

This JSON structure maintains the semi-structured nature of the data, allowing for flexibility while following JSON formatting.

Pros and cons of semi-structured data

One of the powerful advantages of this type of data management is that it is not constrained by fixed schema and is flexible for changes to objects. It supports the heterogeneous nature of the sources and allows users to represent their data needs in NoSQL format. It is highly scalable and quicker because its nature makes indexing and querying much easier and flexible.

As with anything, semi-structured data format also comes with its cons. Since there is no support for a fixed form of schema or storage, identifying relationships between data is difficult and querying is relatively inefficient. Since this kind of data has several sources, it is complex to manage and has far less support in terms of tools and technologies that can handle the use cases. Security issues can arise from storing data in the form of tags and XML, as the nested, unstructured portions of the data might contain sensitive information.

Let's look at a few use cases to understand the real-world usage of semi-structured data.

Use cases of semi-structured data

Semi-structured data is produced in several real-world applications including the following:

- **Internet of Things (IoT) sensors in manufacturing**: Semi-structured data from remote IoT sensors is used to derive actionable insights and optimize operations in manufacturing

- **Industrial automation and robotics**: It helps automate industrial processes and control robotic systems efficiently

- **Healthcare**: Semi-structured data plays a crucial role in healthcare for managing patient data and medical records

- **Wearable sports and fitness devices**: Data from wearables helps individuals track their fitness and sports performance

- **Web-based content**: Semi-structured data on the web with diverse markup schemas is essential for collecting and analyzing online content

- **E-commerce**: In e-commerce, it's used to manage product catalogs and customer data

- **Finance**: It's employed for tracking web behavioral data in finance, aiding in risk assessment and fraud detection

- **Engagement and adoption analytics**: In software products, semi-structured data is utilized to analyze user engagement and adoption patterns

- **Social media analytics**: Semi-structured data from social media platforms is leveraged for sentiment analysis, user engagement metrics, and marketing insights

- **Search engines and information retrieval**: In the field of search engines and information retrieval, semi-structured data helps index and retrieve web content efficiently, improving search accuracy and relevance

These are only some use cases that highlight the diverse applications of semi-structured data across various industries and domains. Managing semi-structured data, as seen in these diverse use cases, often involves leveraging NoSQL databases and efficient indexing methods to handle the inherent flexibility and complexity of this data.

NoSQL for semi-structured data

NoSQL is a type of database management system that is designed to cater to the needs of semi-structured and unstructured forms of data modeled in formats other than the tabular one supported by relational databases. NoSQL databases are mainly used to manage big data and real-time web applications. You can think of NoSQL as a system or language that not only supports SQL but also unstructured and semi-structured queries and data. The objective of NoSQL databases can be simply put as follows:

- Robust and simple design
- Flexible in terms of format and source
- Object-oriented application—database dependency limitation
- Better control over availability
- Partition tolerance

NoSQL databases adhere to the CAP theorem, which guarantees two of the following three principles for any distributed data store:

- **Consistency**: This is different from the consistency addressed by the **atomicity, consistency, isolation, and durability** (ACID) principles followed by the relational database management systems. Here, it means that every data read receives the most recently updated data or an error.
- **Availability**: Every request receives a response. Whether it is recent or not might not be guaranteed.
- **Partition Tolerance**: This means that the system continues to respond to requests even when there is network partition failure by doing one of two things:
  - Canceling the operation and ensuring a high consistency but lower availability
  - Continuing the operation and providing availability over consistency

So, such systems mandate a choice of consistency or availability if partitions are part of the design, but if there are no partitions, both consistency and availability can be satisfied.

Data structures supported by NoSQL databases

NoSQL can be further categorized broadly into the following four data structures. Some databases support each of these data structure types:

- **Document store**: Document databases store data in a format similar to the JSON document data type, storing data as pairs of fields and values. The values themselves have the flexibility of being in a variety of data structures. With the increased usage of JSON, document databases have gained increased popularity in web application design.

- **Key-value**: Key-value databases pair keys with their associated values. Owing to their simplicity, they are extremely useful in scenarios that need high scalability and performance. Discretely ordered keys in the key-value model can prove to be computationally powerful in terms of retrieval of key ranges.

- **Wide-column**: Wide-column databases follow the table structure in the form of rows and columns similar to relational databases, except that as opposed to row-oriented storage, wide-column databases store columns separately. It proves very effective for use cases and applications that require querying column by column.

- **Graph**: Graph databases store data points and relationships between two data points. The data points are referred to as nodes and relationships are referred to as edges. Since these databases store the relationships between nodes, they are mostly applied in use cases that require the representation of complex hierarchies and relationships in data, such as social network sites and customer relationship representation applications.

Some examples of NoSQL databases are Google Cloud Firestore, Cloud Bigtable, MongoDB, CouchDB, Neo4j, and DynamoDB. Firestore and Cloud Bigtable are Google Cloud NoSQL offerings, and both databases are fully managed. Cloud Bigtable is a petabyte-scale wide-column database that powers many core Google services, such as Search, Analytics, Gmail, and Maps.

In the upcoming sections, we will cover some feature highlights and the hands-on fundamentals of setting up a Firestore database for a sample application.

> **Note:**
>
> Please be advised that certain features and services described in the following sections may have undergone modifications since the time of drafting. The screenshots may look different from what you see in the book. APIs and versions may have been updated by the time you are reading this. As such, kindly exercise flexibility and adapt your steps accordingly.
>
> Additionally, some services may incur charges if they are outside the free tier (if applicable). Therefore, it is recommended to be aware of the services you are enabling and to delete or deactivate services and instances that are no longer required for learning or demonstration purposes.

Firestore and its features

Firestore is a serverless document database that scales easily and flexibly to meet any growing demand with no maintenance. In the Firestore database, data is stored as documents that are organized into collections. Documents contain subcollections, nested objects, and complex objects such as lists. If you don't start by creating a collection or document for your use case, Firestore automatically creates it as needed. The following are some key features that stand out to me in using Firestore as a document database:

- Firestore, being fully managed and serverless, allows developers to focus fully on application development and effortlessly scale up and down without any maintenance or downtime.

- Since it supports live sync and offline mode, it is ideal for mobile and web applications in several real-time use cases and remote low-accessibility situations.

- The powerful query engine allows you to run ACID transactions on document data.

- It offers support for several client libraries and server-side libraries.

- It has customizable identity-based access controls and integration with the Firebase authentication and identity platform.

- It has automatic multi-region replication support.

- Strong consistency and high availability (99.999%, which is the best in the industry) are guaranteed. Strong consistency is a property of a database system that ensures that when data is read from the database after a write operation, the read will always return the most recent and up-to-date version of the data. In other words, if multiple users or applications are accessing and modifying the same data concurrently, strong consistency guarantees that every read operation will reflect the effects of all previous write operations in the order they were performed. This level of consistency is crucial for applications where data accuracy and correctness are paramount, such as financial systems or critical healthcare databases. However, achieving strong consistency can sometimes come at the cost of increased latency or reduced availability, as the database system may need to wait for acknowledgments from multiple servers to ensure consistency. High availability in a database system refers to its ability to remain operational and accessible even in the face of hardware failures, network issues, or other unforeseen events. It is achieved through redundancy and fault-tolerant design. High availability ensures that users and applications can continue to interact with the database and retrieve data even when some components of the system are experiencing problems. Firestore, for instance, provides high availability through data replication across multiple data centers or regions. This means that even if one data center or server becomes unavailable, the system can continue to serve requests from other available locations, minimizing downtime and ensuring uninterrupted access to data.

In the next section, we will learn how to set up your application-supporting document data to use the Firestore database for operations.

Setting up Firestore

If you are new to Google Cloud, first of all, go to Google Cloud Console (`https://console.cloud.google.com/`), select your organization, and create a new Google Cloud project with billing enabled.

You can follow the instructions here:

`https://cloud.google.com/resource-manager/docs/creating-managing-projects`

All the following steps can be done with Command Shell commands or in Google Cloud Console:

1. In the Google Cloud Console, search for Firestore in the search bar.

2. From the **Firestore Viewer** page, in the **Select a cloud Firestore mode** screen, select **Firestore in Native mode**: https://console.cloud.google.com/firestore/.

3. Select a location for your Firestore data. Remember that this choice is permanent.

4. Click on **Create database**.

5. When you create the Firestore project, the Firestore API is enabled.

6. Once you set this up, you should be able to see the database, collection, and document view where you can add the collection, document, and subcollection, as represented in the following figure:

Figure 6.1 – Firestore Data panel view

This figure represents the structure of the data stored in the Firestore collection poses, its documents (the selected document is halasana), and its subcollection fitness_part.

In *Figure 6.1*, the object underlined by a black line is the collection that acts as containers for the documents. The one underlined in red refers to the documents that are contained within a collection. Then, for each document, there are fields represented by key-values, underlined in blue. Documents can also contain subcollections, which you can find underlined in green.

The following figure shows the structure of the fitness_part subcollection, its spine document, and its corresponding field:

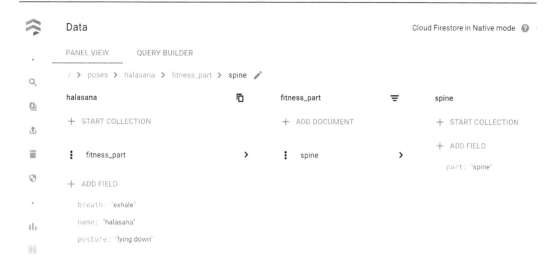

Figure 6.2 – Firestore Data Panel View showing the subcollection fitness_part

Let's discuss the components of this dataset in detail.

Collection

Collections contain documents and nothing more. Collections cannot contain raw fields and values or other collections. In the sample record, we created in the preceding figure, poses is the collection, and it is supposed to contain different Yoga postures as its documents.

Document

Documents are lightweight JSON records, and they contain data in key-value pairs of different data types. They can contain subcollections, nested objects, primitive type fields, complex objects (such as lists), and maps. In our sample record, we have a document under poses named halasana. It has the breath, name, and posture keys with respective values of exhale, halasana, and lying down.

Subcollection

Subcollections are collections associated with a specific document, and they allow the data to be structured hierarchically and nested. In our sample record, under the halasana pose, we have created a collection named fitness_part, which is the subcollection that has the document with the part key and the value of spine.

Now that we have understood the components of the semi-structured dataset in Firestore, let's move on to other key design aspects.

Security

After we have configured the database and set up sample collections and objects, it is important to provision security rules for your data to control access. Firestore offers two types of security, authentication, and access control methods depending on your choice of client libraries:

- **Mobile and web client libraries**: These are Firebase authentication and security rules that perform serverless authentication, authorization, and data validation

- **Server client libraries**: **Identity and access management (IAM)** is a method of access control for your database

You should be able to create, edit, and monitor security rules easily from the Firebase interface. Follow this link to get started: `https://cloud.google.com/firestore/docs/security/get-started`.

You can read more about it in this documentation: `https://cloud.google.com/firestore/docs/security/overview`.

Remember to always test and monitor your security rules before deploying or rolling out your application from the development phase.

Client libraries and APIs

Firestore supports several mobile and web SDKs, server client libraries, Admin SDKs, Google Cloud client libraries, REST APIs, and other third-party library integrations.

Reference their documentation for finding your language or platform-specific sample and library in the documentation:

`https://cloud.google.com/firestore/docs/reference/libraries`

If you'd like to try out a sample web application that I built using Firestore REST API on a Java Spring Boot framework, check out this project:

`https://github.com/AbiramiSukumaran/firestore-project`

Indexing

A database index helps connect items to their locations. It is used to improve the speed of search in queries. If the index does not exist, databases typically search for items one by one. But Firestore supports high-performance queries by indexing all your queries, which means the following:

- Indexes for your basic queries are all automatically created for you

- Query performance is dependent on query results and not on the record volume in the database

- There are the two types of indexes:

    - A **single-field index** is an ordered mapping of all the documents in a collection consisting of a specific field

    - A **composite index** is also an ordered mapping of documents, but it is based on an ordered list of fields to index (basically field-combinations as opposed to one specific field)

- A **collection group query** refers to the hierarchy of collections, documents, subcollections, and so on, and querying such collection groups is possible through collection group indexes

Let's look at these indexes in a little more detail.

Single-field index

A single-field index in Firestore is a database index created on a single field within a document:

- It is used to optimize queries that involve filtering, sorting, or ordering data based on a specific field.

- Single-field indexes are automatically created for fields (and subfields) you query on, but you can also create custom single-field indexes for frequently used fields to improve query performance.

- Firestore allows querying for documents based on equality, inequality, or range conditions using single-field indexes.

- Single-field indexes are essential for efficiently retrieving data and are a fundamental part of Firestore's query performance optimization.

- You can also choose to create a single-field index exemption to exclude any field from your automatic index settings. It also overrides the database-wide default indexing setting.

The following figure shows single-field indexes created for the collection we created:

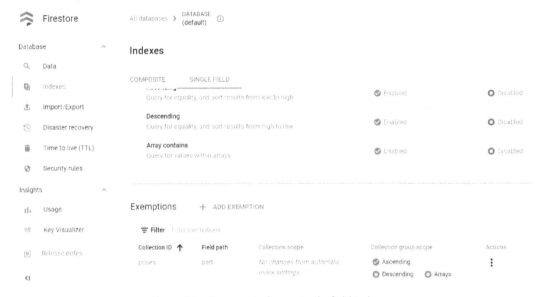

Figure 6.3 – Firestore Indexes: single-field indexes

As you can see in the figure, a single-field index has been created for all fields, one for each (ascending, descending, and array contain queries), automatically enabling most simple queries by default. You can also note that in the **Exemptions** section, you can exclude fields from the automatic index settings.

Composite index

A composite index in Firestore is an index that combines multiple fields within a document to optimize complex queries. It has the following properties:

- It is used when you need to filter or sort data based on multiple fields simultaneously.

- Composite indexes are manually created, and Firestore requires you to define them explicitly for compound queries involving more than one field.

- These indexes help Firestore execute complex queries efficiently by reducing the need to scan all documents and enabling faster data retrieval.

- When you attempt to execute a compound query without a pre-existing composite index, Firestore will prompt you to create one to ensure query performance.

- You can also choose to create a single-field index exemption to exclude any field from your automatic index settings. It also overrides the database-wide default indexing setting.

The following figure shows composite indexes created for the collection we created:

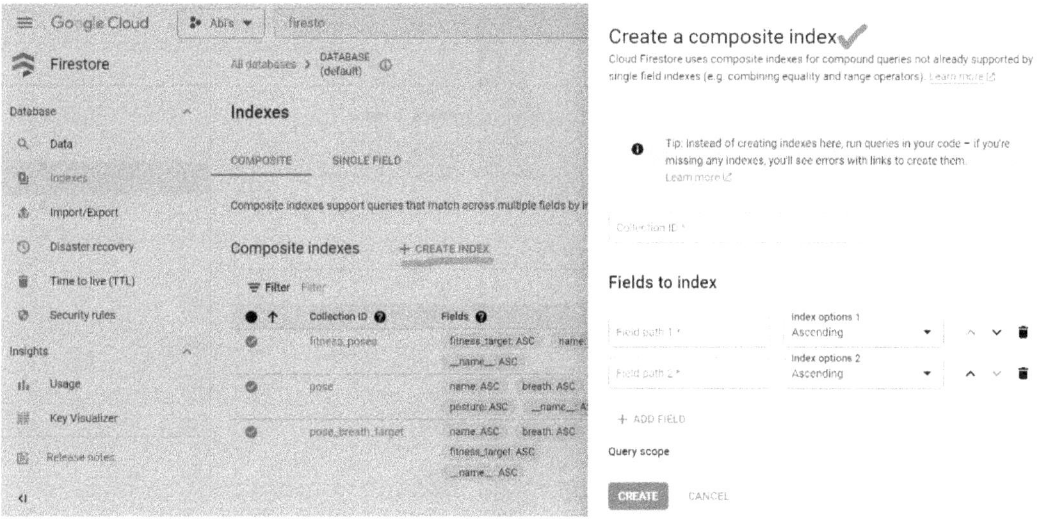

Figure 6.4 – Firestore Indexes: composite indexes

As you can see in the figure, the composite indexes that I created are already listed in the composite indexes section. You can create a new composite index by clicking the **CREATE INDEX** button and entering the details required in the **Create a composite index** popup.

Collection group query

A collection group query is a powerful feature in Firestore that allows you to query across multiple collections with the same name:

- It is used when you want to search for documents in multiple collections with similar structures
- Collection group queries are handy for scenarios such as retrieving all user comments from various subcollections or accessing data distributed across different parts of your database
- These queries enable you to efficiently search and aggregate data across collections with a common name, making it easier to work with related data spread across your Firestore database
- Collection group queries are performed by specifying the collection name as a target and can be combined with filters and sorting to retrieve the desired data
- If a query is executed without the required index in place, Firestore fails it and provides a link to create the index automatically

The following figure shows the collection group query option for the collection we created:

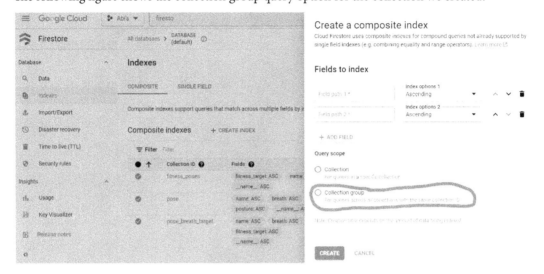

Figure 6.5 – Firestore Indexes: Collection group option

As you can see in this figure, in the **Create a composite index** pop-up, you can choose the **Collection group** option to enable queries across all collections with the same collection ID.

Firestore's indexing, including single-field and composite indexes, and collection group queries empower developers to efficiently retrieve and manipulate data in a flexible and scalable manner while maintaining control over query performance.

Data model considerations

When it comes to the data model design choice, we always struggle to choose between a hierarchical (collection group) format and a format closer to a denormalized form (top-level collection) of storing data. Before we get into that, let's talk about the hierarchical and denormalized formats!

Hierarchical format

The hierarchical format represents information in a structured, nested format. This format is ideal for scenarios where data has clear parent–child relationships or when you want to maintain a well-defined structure. The following is an example of hierarchical data using JSON to represent an organizational hierarchy:

```
{
  "organization": {
    "name": "XYZ Corporation",
    "departments": [
```

```
    {
        "name": "HR",
        "employees": [
            {
                "name": "Alice",
                "position": "HR Manager"
            },
            {
                "name": "Bob",
                "position": "HR Specialist"
            }
        ]
    },
    {
        "name": "Engineering",
        "employees": [
            {
                "name": "Charlie",
                "position": "Engineering Manager"
            },
            {
                "name": "David",
                "position": "Software Engineer"
            }
        ]
    }
    ]
  }
]
}
```

Denormalized format

The denormalized format combines related data into a single structure to optimize for read operations and reduce the need for complex joins in database queries. It's often used in scenarios where read performance is critical, but it can result in data duplication. The following is an example of denormalized data in a database table for an e-commerce website:

```
[
    {
        "order_id": 1,
        "customer_name": "Alice",
        "product_name": "Widget A",
        "quantity": 5,
```

```
    "price": 10.99,
    "order_date": "2023-10-06"
  },
  {
    "order_id": 2,
    "customer_name": "Bob",
    "product_name": "Gadget B",
    "quantity": 3,
    "price": 19.95,
    "order_date": "2023-10-07"
  }
]
```

In this denormalized JSON structure, each object represents an order with all relevant data, including customer information and product information, combined into a single structure. This approach optimizes read operations because all the required data is readily available in each object. However, it may result in data redundancy if multiple orders share the same customer or product details.

The choice depends on your business requirements. But remember the following:

- If you are going to query your documents with a common parent and expect to rarely use the cross-collection query, go with the subcollection collection group format and enable collection group indexes as the scope for your query
- If your application involves a lot of cross-collection query, choose the top-level collection structure as the scope for your query

Now that we have learned hands-on how to set up and create a Firestore database and understood its components, indexes, and data model design consideration, let's find out how to query semi-structured data using the RunQuery API method that Firestore offers.

Easy querying with RunQuery API

Firestore offers a straightforward way to query your data using a REST API-based mechanism called the RunQuery API. This API allows you to retrieve specific data from your Firestore database using HTTP requests.

API endpoint and method

To use the RunQuery API, you make a POST request to the following endpoint:

```
https://firestore.googleapis.com/v1/{parent=projects/*/databases/*/
documents}:runQuery
```

The parent parameter

In the API request, you'll need to provide the `parent` parameter with a value in this format:

```
projects/{project_id}/databases/{databaseId}/documents
```

Replace `{project_id}` and `{databaseId}` with your specific project and database identifiers.

JSON body format

The request body should be in JSON format and include the `structuredQuery` object, which defines the specifics of your query. The `structuredQuery` object contains various query parameters, such as `select`, `from`, `where`, `orderBy`, `startAt`, `endAt`, `offset`, and `limit`.

The JSON body format is as follows:

```
{
  "structuredQuery": {
    object (StructuredQuery)
  },
  // Union field consistency_selector can be only one of the
following:
  "transaction": string,
  "newTransaction": {
    object (TransactionOptions)
  },
  "readTime": string
  // End of list of possible types for union field consistency_
selector.
}
```

StructuredQuery

The `StructuredQuery` section is where you define your query using a JSON object with specific fields:

- `select`: This specifies which fields or projections you want to retrieve
- `from`: This identifies the collections or documents you want to query from
- `where`: This allows you to set filter conditions for your query
- `orderBy`: This specifies the sorting order for the results
- `startAt` and `endAt`: These define the cursors to paginate through results
- `offset` and `limit`: These control the number of results returned and the starting point for pagination

The structure of `StructuredQuery` is as follows:

```
{
  "select": { object (Projection) },
  "from": [ {  object (CollectionSelector)   } ],
  "where": { object (Filter)  },
  "orderBy": [  { object (Order)  } ],
  "startAt": { object (Cursor) },
  "endAt": { object (Cursor) },
  "offset": integer,
  "limit": integer
}
```

The from clause

Within the `from` clause, you specify the collection or document you want to query from. The `collectionId` parameter indicates the collection name, and `allDescendants` is a Boolean flag that determines whether to include documents from all descendant collections:

```
{
  "collectionId": string,
  "allDescendants": boolean
}
```

The where clause

The `where` clause allows you to filter your query based on specific criteria. It comprises three main components:

- `Object`: This represents the field you want to filter on
- `Op`: This defines the operator (e.g., equality, inequality) for comparison
- `Value`: This specifies the value you want to compare the field against

Putting the pieces together

Putting them together, let us construct a sample JSON input for our `poses` collection:

```
{
  "structuredQuery": {
    "select":
    {
      "fields":   [
      {
```

```
        "fieldPath": "name"
      },
      {
        "fieldPath": "breath"
      },
      {
        "fieldPath": "posture"
      }
    ]
  },
    "from": [{
          "collectionId": "poses"
      }
    ]
  }
}
```

We have written an HTTP RunQuery method query input for selecting the field name, breath, and posture from the poses collection without any where clause filter condition.

To test this, let's create a simple curl command with a POST method to the URL we created:

```
curl --header "Content-Type: application/json" \
  --request POST \
  --data '{"structuredQuery": {"select":{"fields":   [{ "fieldPath":
"name"}, { "fieldPath": "breath"}, { "fieldPath": "posture" }] },
"from": [{"collectionId": "poses" } ] } } ' \
"https://firestore.googleapis.com/v1/projects/<<YOUR_PROJECT_ID>>/
databases/(default)/documents:runQuery"
```

Click on the **Activate Cloud Shell** icon (circled in *Figure 6.6*) to open the Cloud Shell terminal. Copy and paste your curl command and hit *Enter* to run the CURL command, as shown here:

Figure 6.6 – Cloud shell terminal with the curl command (1)

You should see the result in the following figure:

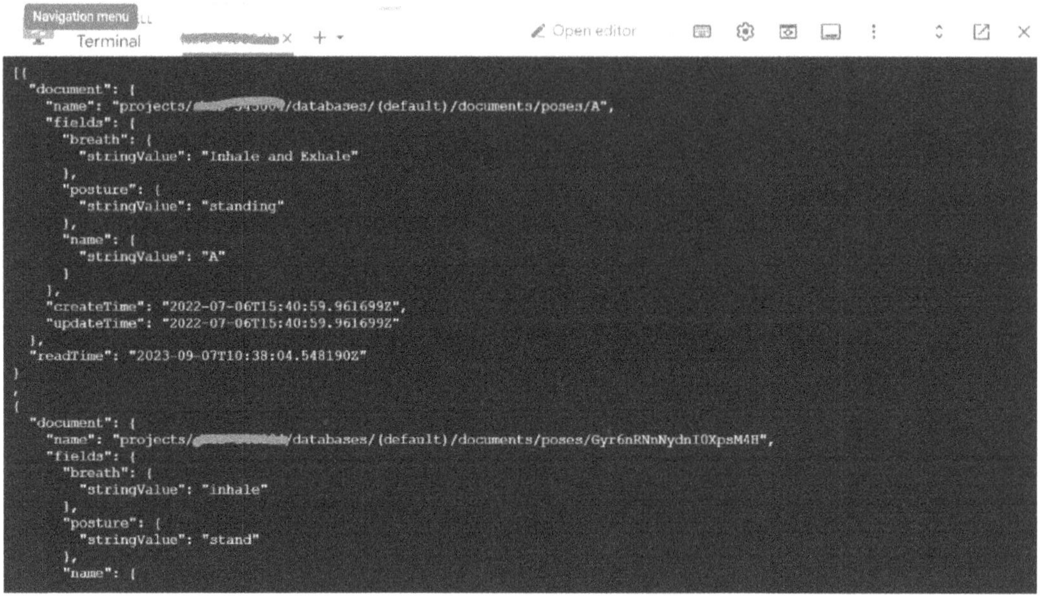

Figure 6.7 – Cloud shell terminal with the curl command (2)

Go ahead and try more queries or modify this query by introducing a `where` clause and check the query results for yourself!

Implementing RunQuery API programmatically

Now, let's invoke this Firestore RunQuery API programmatically by implementing this in a standalone application that is deployed serverlessly on Google Cloud. After reading *Chapter 4, Setting Up a Fully Managed RDBMS*, you should be familiar with the steps involved in setting up Cloud Functions. If not, go to the *Create an application with the cloud database* section in *Chapter 4, Setting Up a Fully Managed RDBMS* and follow the instructions to create a Java Cloud Functions application.

Replace the `pom.xml` dependencies section with the following dependencies to include the libraries required for this implementation:

```
<dependency>
    <groupId>com.google.cloud.functions</groupId>
    <artifactId>functions-framework-api</artifactId>
    <version>1.0.4</version>
  </dependency>
<dependency>
  <groupId>org.springframework</groupId>
```

```
    <artifactId>spring-web</artifactId>
    <version>5.0.2.RELEASE</version>
</dependency>
```

Replace the HelloHttpFunction.java class with the following code. This is the class in which we will implement the Firestore RunQuery API invocation to execute the SELECT statement programmatically:

```
package gcfv2;
import java.io.BufferedWriter;
import com.google.cloud.functions.HttpFunction;
import com.google.cloud.functions.HttpRequest;
import com.google.cloud.functions.HttpResponse;
import org.springframework.http.HttpHeaders;
import org.springframework.http.MediaType;
import org.springframework.http.HttpEntity;
import org.springframework.http.ResponseEntity;
import org.springframework.http.RequestEntity;
import org.springframework.http.HttpMethod;
import org.springframework.web.client.RestTemplate;
import java.util.Arrays;


/*
This is the HelloHttpFunction class that implements the HttpFunction
interface.
*/
public class HelloHttpFunction implements HttpFunction {
  public void service(final HttpRequest request, final HttpResponse
response) throws Exception {
    final BufferedWriter writer = response.getWriter();
/*
Call the callURL method that has the API invocation steps.
*/
    writer.write(callURL());
  }
/*
The callURL() method calls the Firestore RunQuery API to execute the
SELECT statement and returns the JSON string with the result of the
query.
*/
public String callURL(){
    try{
        String paramString = "https://firestore.googleapis.com/v1/
projects/<<YOUR_PROJECT_ID>>/databases/(default)/documents:runQuery";
        String jsonString = "{\"structuredQuery\":
{\"select\":{\"fields\":  [{ \"fieldPath\": \"name\"}, {
```

```
\"fieldPath\": \"breath\"}, { \"fieldPath\": \"posture\" }] },
\"from\": [{\"collectionId\": \"poses\" } ] } }";
        System.out.println("paramString: " + paramString);
        System.out.println("JSON: " + jsonString);
        HttpHeaders headers = new HttpHeaders();
        headers.setAccept(Arrays.asList(MediaType.APPLICATION_JSON));
        HttpEntity<String> entity = new HttpEntity<>(jsonString,
headers);
    RestTemplate restTemplate = new RestTemplate();
        ResponseEntity<String> result = restTemplate.
exchange(paramString, HttpMethod.POST, entity, String.class);
        System.out.println(result);
        return result.toString();
        }catch(Exception e){
            System.out.println("EXCEPTION in edit" + e);
            return "errmessage";
        }
    }
}
```

Click the **DEPLOY** button to deploy it and get the HTTPS REST endpoint for the serverless Cloud Function. Click the URL and see the query result as a JSON string in your browser, as shown here:

{ "document": { "name": "projects/abis-345004/databases/(default)/documents/poses/A", "fields": { "breath": { "stringValue": "Inhale and Exhale" }, "posture": { "stringValue": "standing" }, "name": { "stringValue": "A" } }, "createTime": "2022-07-06T15:40:59.961699Z", "updateTime": "2022-07-06T15:40:59.961699Z" }, "readTime": "2023-11-28T16:38:47.295724Z" } , { "document": { "name": "projects/abis-345004/databases/(default)/documents/poses/Gyr6nRNnNydnIOXpsM4H", "fields": { "breath": { "stringValue": "inhale" }, "posture": { "stringValue": "stand" }, "name": { "stringValue": "urdhvahastasana" } }, "createTime": "2022-06-28T20:22:08.848465Z", "updateTime": "2022-06-28T20:22:08.848465Z" }, "readTime": "2023-11-28T16:38:47.295724Z" } , { "document": { "name": "projects/abis-345004/databases/(default)/documents/poses/Uttanasana", "fields": { "breath": { "stringValue": "Exhale" }, "posture": { "stringValue": "Standing" }, "name": { "stringValue": "Uttanasana" } }, "createTime": "2022-07-08T05:16:38.742451Z", "updateTime": "2022-07-08T05:16:38.742451Z" }, "readTime": "2023-11-28T16:38:47.295724Z" } , { "document": { "name": "projects/abis-345004/databases/(default)/documents/poses/halasana", "fields": { "breath": { "stringValue": "exhale" }, "posture": { "stringValue": "lying down" }, "name": { "stringValue": "halasana" } }, "createTime": "2022-07-06T14:49:51.978409Z", "updateTime": "2022-07-06T14:49:51.978409Z" }, "readTime": "2023-11-28T16:38:47.295724Z" } , { "document": { "name": "projects/abis-345004/databases/(default)/documents/poses/rZ5ScqSfxwzPMvi474rH", "fields": { "breath": { "stringValue": "exhale" }, "posture": { "stringValue": "stand" }, "name": { "stringValue": "tadasana" } }, "createTime": "2022-06-28T20:19:53.884013Z", "updateTime": "2022-06-28T20:19:53.884013Z" }, "readTime": "2023-11-28T16:38:47.295724Z" } , { "document": { "name": "projects/abis-345004/databases/(default)/documents/poses/tadasana", "fields": { "breath": { "stringValue": "Inhale and Exhale" }, "posture": { "stringValue": "stand" }, "name": { "stringValue": "tadasana" } }, "createTime": "2022-07-02T09:32:10.030550Z", "updateTime": "2022-07-06T13:59:35.428101Z" }, "readTime": "2023-11-28T16:38:47.295724Z" } , { "document": { "name": "projects/abis-345004/databases/(default)/documents/poses/urdhvahastasana", "fields": { "breath": { "stringValue": "inhale" }, "posture": { "stringValue": "stand" }, "name": { "stringValue": "urdhvahastasana" } }, "createTime": "2022-07-02T09:31:56.581197Z", "updateTime": "2022-07-02T09:31:56.581197Z" }, "readTime": "2023-11-28T16:38:47.295724Z" } , { "document": { "name": "projects/abis-345004/databases/(default)/documents/poses/virabadrasana", "fields": { "breath": { "stringValue": "exhale" }, "posture": { "stringValue": "standing" }, "name": { "stringValue": "virabadrasana" } }, "createTime": "2022-07-06T14:50:22.496329Z", "updateTime": "2022-07-06T14:50:22.496329Z" }, "readTime": "2023-11-28T16:38:47.295724Z" }

Figure 6.8 – JSON response for the query invoked in a Cloud Function

Feel free to process the JSON and use it in your application. Also, as an exercise, try including the where clause and other constructs in your query.

Summary

In this chapter, we explored semi-structured data and its fundamental aspects, real-world use cases, and design considerations. Semi-structured data, characterized by its adaptability and hierarchical nature, bridges the gap between structured and unstructured data, making it an invaluable resource in today's data-driven landscape.

We then talked about NoSQL databases, which are designed to handle semi-structured and unstructured data efficiently. These databases prioritize robust design, flexibility, and high availability. We explored the principles of consistency, availability, and partition tolerance, which are crucial for distributed data stores.

Firestore, a serverless document database, stood out as a prime example of a NoSQL database. Its features, including scalability, strong consistency, and multi-region replication, make it a top choice for various applications. The chapter also shed light on Firestore's data model, indexing techniques, and collection group queries, which enable developers to optimize data retrieval while maintaining control over query performance.

As we wrap up this chapter, remember that the choice between hierarchical and denormalized data models depends on your specific business needs. Whether you choose subcollections or top-level collections, Firestore offers powerful querying capabilities through its RunQuery API, as demonstrated in our practical examples.

With a solid understanding of semi-structured data and Firestore's capabilities, you are well-equipped to utilize flexible data structures in your applications. I encourage you to build a simple web application and integrate it with the data model we just created.

In the upcoming chapter, we will learn all about unstructured data, its storage, and its design considerations.

7
Unstructured Data Management

Unstructured data is said to constitute a huge portion of data generated today. Some industry studies say at least 85% of data available today is unstructured. So, what is this unstructured data? Data with no predefined external structure in the form of a schema or table (rows and columns), object structure (JSON, XML, and so on), or data model is termed unstructured data, even though such data can have an internal structure. It can be generated by machines, humans, or applications.

Some common examples and sources of unstructured data are images, audio, video, files, and rich media. The fact that it is not constrained by fixed schema and is flexible for analyzing and drawing insights from raw data as-is is one of the major advantages of this type of data management. However, industries and organizations are not able to take full advantage of data of this kind for many reasons:

- The complexity involved in terms of data storage, management, processing, analytics, and inference
- Limited availability of infrastructure and resources required to handle the integration of such unstructured data with the existing applications and data
- Unavailability of talent and expertise required to handle this management and integration
- Scaling (a few bytes to terabytes) and high availability become a challenge as the data grows exponentially and the unconventional methods and sources from which the data is ingested
- Querying, performing basic analytics, advanced machine learning, and prediction become difficult with the unconventional formats, size, and volume of unstructured data

So, how can we prepare to use this kind of data in applications? That is exactly what we will discuss in detail here while covering the following topics:

- Use cases and real-world applications
- Services available for processing unstructured data
- Diving deep into Google Cloud Storage for storing and managing unstructured data

- Storing and managing unstructured data with BigQuery

- Analytics and insights into unstructured data with BigQuery

We will discuss these topics by providing real-world examples and step-by-step guides to hands-on exercises, similar to what we've done previously in this book.

Use cases

Unstructured data is generated in the real world in the form of social media posts, tweets, IoT data, camera feeds, movies, music, AI-generated data, and more. Organizations and businesses can use this kind of data to solve problems transactionally and also to derive analytical insights. Some transactional applications use unstructured data for the following reasons:

- Verify biometric information such as facial recognition for checked-in passengers in airports

- Process music and video files to identify songs, videos, and faces

- Image classification and identification

- Video and audio suggestions and personalization

- Behavior-based usage prediction

- Behavior-based fraud detection

- Posture detection and tracking in sports and fitness applications

- Movement and symptoms-based health alert generation and tracking

Analytical applications for unstructured data are unlimited as organizations have the potential to scale, evolve, and transform their businesses with the analysis and insights from unstructured data.

Processing unstructured data

Unstructured data can be stored and managed as-is in object storage services. However, the problem with object storage is the cost and complexity involved in the storage, access, and archival strategy for unstructured data. Since most applications that use unstructured data involve searching, we also have to think about indexing options for such forms of data. Depending on the type of unstructured data you want to store (files, blocks of VMs or databases, images, videos, and so on), the type of application you are dealing with for processing (mobile apps, analytical apps, transactional web applications, and so on) and the purpose of its usage (storage, archival, backup and disaster recovery and transfer, and so on), there are several services of unstructured data to choose from.

In the next section, we will look at some of the Google Cloud options available for unstructured data design.

Storage options in Google Cloud

In Google Cloud, there are several options for unstructured data storage, depending on your requirements, format, and purpose of application or storage. Let's look at a few:

- **Cloud Storage**: Cloud Storage is a fully managed object storage service in Google Cloud that allows you to store any type, duration, and volume of data. It is mainly used in service use cases such as streaming videos, images for web applications, and data storage in data lakes.

- **Filestore**: It is a fully managed high-performance service for file storage that supports high-performance scalability, high availability, backup, and security.

- **Block Storage**: It is a fully managed, high-performance persistent disk for virtual machines. High scalability, pay-per-use, high flexibility, and high performance are some of the key features of Block Storage.

- **Storage Transfer Service**: To transfer data across multiple services and service providers quickly and securely, Google Cloud provides Storage Transfer Service or Data Transfer Service, which moves data from cloud to cloud, on-premises to the cloud, and between Cloud Storage buckets.

- **BigQuery**: BigQuery allows you to store, reference, query, and perform analytics on unstructured data (images, videos, and so on) by integrating smoothly with Cloud Storage using external connection and object table (external table) features. This means that besides being able to take advantage of the fact that you can query structured, semi-structured, and unstructured data independently, you can unify and integrate this data under one roof (BigQuery). This opens up new opportunities for businesses to take advantage of handling all formats of data together, easing the integration step and also improving the precision and accuracy of **machine learning (ML)** and advanced analytics results.

In this chapter, we will cover two of my favorite fully managed Google Cloud services for handling unstructured data storage and management. Besides being my absolute favorites, there is another reason for these services to have been shortlisted in the discussion here: since we are focusing on databases and data modeling in this book, I want to deep dive into SQL-driven application options, irrespective of the structure and type of your data source.

> **Note:**
>
> Please be advised that certain features and services described in the following sections may have undergone modifications since the time of drafting. The screenshots may look different from what you see in the book. APIs and versions may have been updated by the time you are reading this. As such, kindly exercise flexibility and adapt your steps accordingly.
>
> Additionally, some services may incur charges if they are outside the free tier (if applicable). Therefore, it is recommended to be aware of the services you are enabling and to delete or deactivate services and instances that are no longer required for learning or demonstration purposes.

Cloud Storage, classes, and features

Cloud Storage is one of the most preferred fully managed services for companies of all sizes to store and retrieve objects that are in an unstructured format. Cloud Storage stores your objects in containers called buckets. Let's take a hands-on journey through this simple and powerful service for handling unstructured objects.

Before we jump into the actual steps, please make sure you complete the following prerequisites:

1. **Set up a Google Cloud Platform account**: If you don't already have one, sign up for a **Google Cloud Platform (GCP)** account at `https://console.cloud.google.com/`. Create a new project or select an existing project to work with. Make sure that billing is enabled for your project. You can follow the instructions here to create a new project or select an existing one: `https://cloud.google.com/resource-manager/docs/creating-managing-projects`.

    All the steps mentioned here can be completed with Command Shell commands or via Google Cloud Console.

2. **Enable APIs**: Next, we need to enable a few APIs. To enable the required APIs in the GCP Console, navigate to the project you've selected:

    A. Go to the **APIs & Services** section.
    B. Click the **ENABLE APIS AND SERVICES** button.
    C. Enable the **Cloud Storage API**, **BigQuery API**, and **BigQuery Connection API** options.

As you progress through this exercise and experiment further, you will have to enable the APIs for all the Google Cloud services you are engaging with. It is pretty self-explanatory to do so when you follow the console prompts.

Follow these steps to create your unstructured objects in Cloud Storage:

1. Open the Google Cloud console and search for `Cloud Storage`, as shown in the following screenshot:

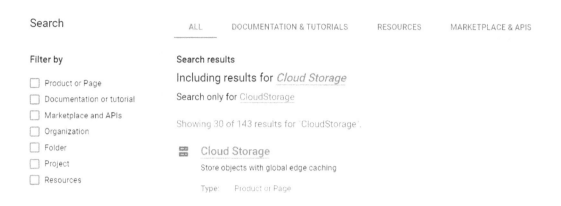

Figure 7.1: Search result for Cloud Storage in the Google Cloud console

2. Go to the **Cloud Storage Buckets** page and click **CREATE**. The **Create a Bucket** page will open, as shown here:

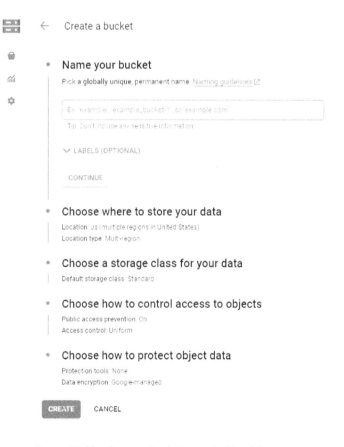

Figure 7.2: The Create a Bucket page in Cloud Storage

3. On the **Create a Bucket** page, enter your preferred bucket name, region, and other details and create it:

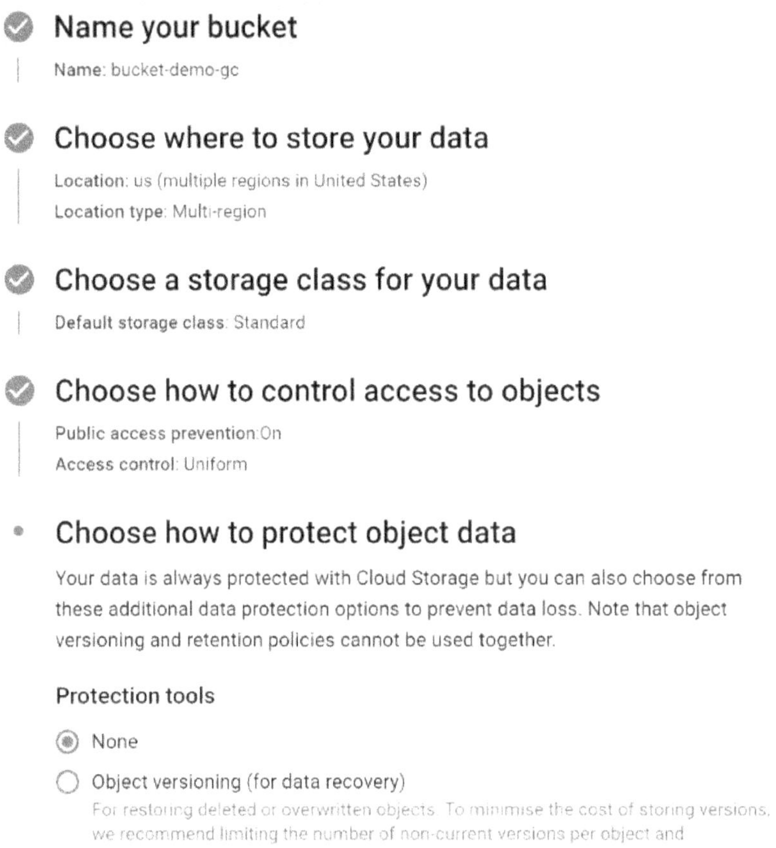

✓ Name your bucket

Name: bucket-demo-gc

✓ Choose where to store your data

Location: us (multiple regions in United States)
Location type: Multi-region

✓ Choose a storage class for your data

Default storage class: Standard

✓ Choose how to control access to objects

Public access prevention:On
Access control: Uniform

• Choose how to protect object data

Your data is always protected with Cloud Storage but you can also choose from these additional data protection options to prevent data loss. Note that object versioning and retention policies cannot be used together.

Protection tools

⦿ None

◯ Object versioning (for data recovery)
For restoring deleted or overwritten objects. To minimise the cost of storing versions, we recommend limiting the number of non-current versions per object and

Figure 7.3: The Create a Bucket page with details entered

4. Once the bucket has been created, you can store your images, videos, and other files inside it by simply clicking the **UPLOAD FILES/UPLOAD FOLDER** option, as shown here:

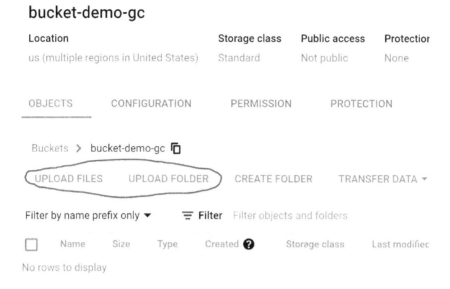

Figure 7.4: The UPLOAD FILES and UPLOAD FOLDER options

5.   Alternatively, you can store your objects in the bucket through Cloud Shell commands or programmatically. The following screenshot shows the **gsutil URI** option for the bucket. You will use this in the Cloud Shell command or your program:

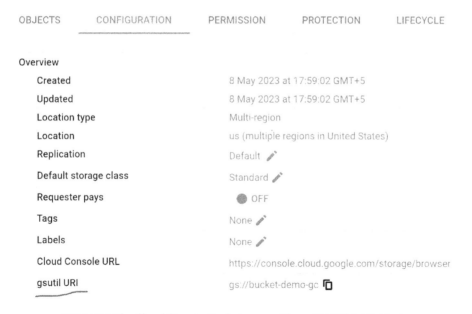

Figure 7.5: The Cloud Storage Bucket page with gsutil URI highlighted

As we can see, the **gsutil URI** part of the bucket we just created (**gs://bucket-demo-gc**) will be used to reference this bucket and the objects it contains in all of its applications.

Cloud Storage supports four classes of storage options:

- **Standard storage**: This storage is used for data that is accessed transactionally and stored for shorter periods of time. It is mostly used by applications streaming videos, audio, websites, and mobile apps.

- **Nearline storage**: This class of storage is for data that is accessed less frequently and that needs to be stored for 30 days. This option is cheaper than the standard storage class.

- **Coldline storage**: Coldline storage is similar to nearline storage in terms of access frequency and is suitable for data that needs to be stored for 90 days. This costs less than coldline storage.

- **Archival storage**: Archival storage is the lowest-cost storage class option available and is suitable for data that can be stored for a year and for archival, backup, and recovery purposes.

Considering your applications' business, functional, and technical requirements, the cost involved, and compliance specifications, you should be able to choose the storage option and configurations that work best for you.

There are some features where Cloud Storage stands out:

- Cloud Storage helps you save costs by allowing automatic storage class transitions. It does this by enabling policy-based automatic object movement to colder storage.

- Cloud Storage has a high replication and short recovery time, so applications can access data in alternate regions in case of outages.

- Configurable security features in terms of access policies, encryption, retention policies, and more.

- Since this storage class keeps your unstructured objects on Google Cloud, it has direct integration with all leading serverless, analytics, and AI/ML services.

- With BigQuery supporting unstructured data storage and analytics, Cloud Storage enables that by connecting to BigQuery using an external connection with BigLake.

In the next section, we will discuss how BigQuery provides a structured way to store and manage unstructured data.

Unstructured data storage with BigQuery

BigQuery supports unstructured data storage and management using object tables. The exciting part for me about this is that you can store unstructured data such as relational data and reference it in rows and columns with structured queries.

External sources

External sources such as Cloud Storage house unstructured data while the data is accessed in BigQuery with metadata fields and references to the unstructured objects. BigQuery uses **object tables** to achieve this. Object tables are read-only tables over unstructured data that you have stored in Cloud Storage. These tables allow you to analyze the unstructured data just like you would do with regular structured data. You can perform analytics and ML, use other ML models on this data, and join the results with structured data in BigQuery. This helps you improve the accuracy of your model, gain deep insights, and make informed decisions based on the combination of structured and unstructured data.

External connections

Object tables are built on BigLake. You need an external connection to connect to and access the objects in Cloud Storage. You can do this with a service account, after which you can access your Cloud Storage data. You can use these connections to perform queries on external data sources without copying the data over to BigQuery. This external connection can be created from the BigQuery console by clicking the **ADD** button in the **Explorer** pane of the BigQuery console:

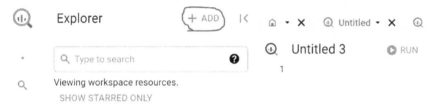

Figure 7.6: The ADD button in the Explorer pane in the BigQuery console

Once you've clicked the **ADD** button (highlighted in the preceding screenshot), click **Connections to external data sources** on the page that opens. This is highlighted in the following screenshot:

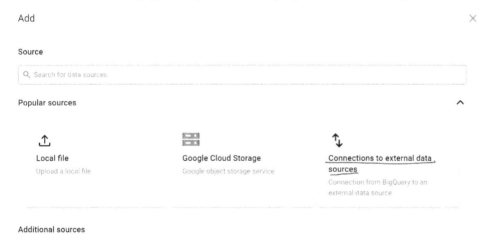

Figure 7.7: Connections to external data sources highlighted in the Add step

Select **BigLake and remote functions (cloud resource)** from the list of options that appear once you click the **Connections to external data sources** option, provide your **Connection ID**, and hit **CREATE CONNECTION**:

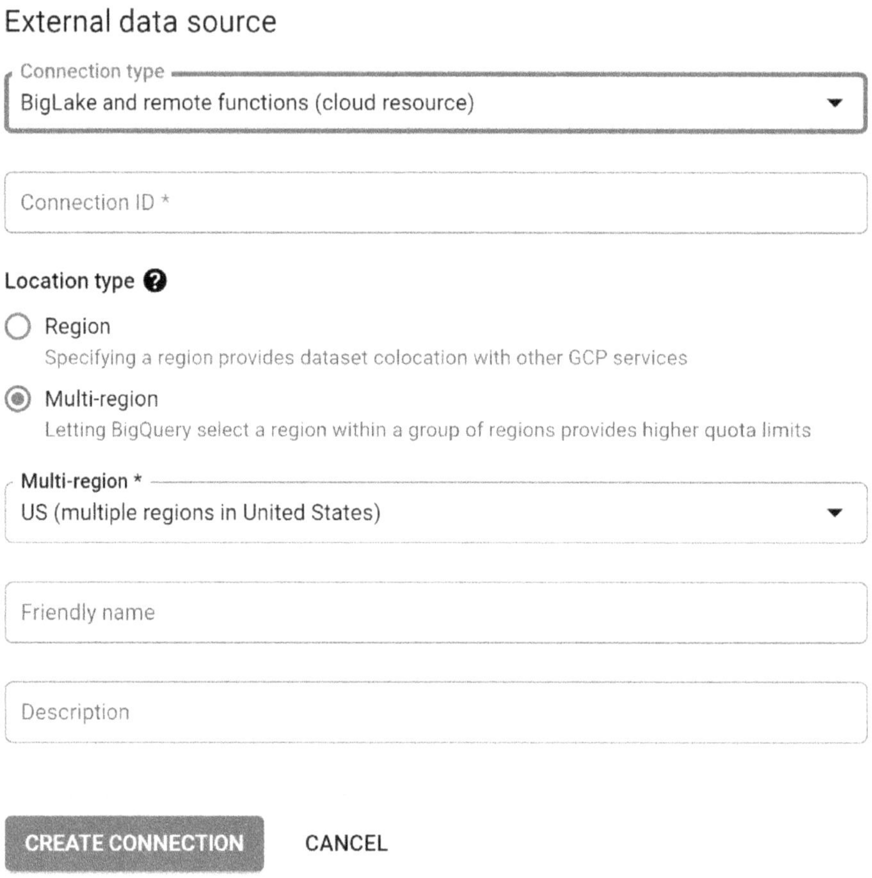

External data source

Connection type
BigLake and remote functions (cloud resource)   ▼

Connection ID *

Location type ❓

⭕ Region
Specifying a region provides dataset colocation with other GCP services

🔘 Multi-region
Letting BigQuery select a region within a group of regions provides higher quota limits

Multi-region *
US (multiple regions in United States)   ▼

Friendly name

Description

CREATE CONNECTION   CANCEL

Figure 7.8: The External data source page showing the CREATE CONNECTION button

Once the connection has been created, go to the newly created connection by clicking on the **GO TO CONNECTION** button as soon as the connection gets created, or by navigating to the **External connections** section under the project in the **Explorer** pane. You can view the **Service account id** details in the **Connection Info** section of the external connection:

Figure 7.9: The Connection Info section

In the next section, we will learn how to store unstructured objects in Cloud Storage buckets and query them from BigQuery using object tables and external connections.

Unstructured data analytics with BigQuery

In this section, we will put the theory of storing unstructured data in BigQuery and querying it into action. If you are wondering why we are storing unstructured data in BigQuery, refer to the *Storage options in BigQuery* section:

1. Go to **Cloud Storage** from the Google Cloud console and select the bucket we created previously (**bucket-demo-gc**).

2. Click **Upload Files** under the **Objects** section and select your files.

3. Once the upload is complete, you should be able to see the files in the bucket, as shown here:

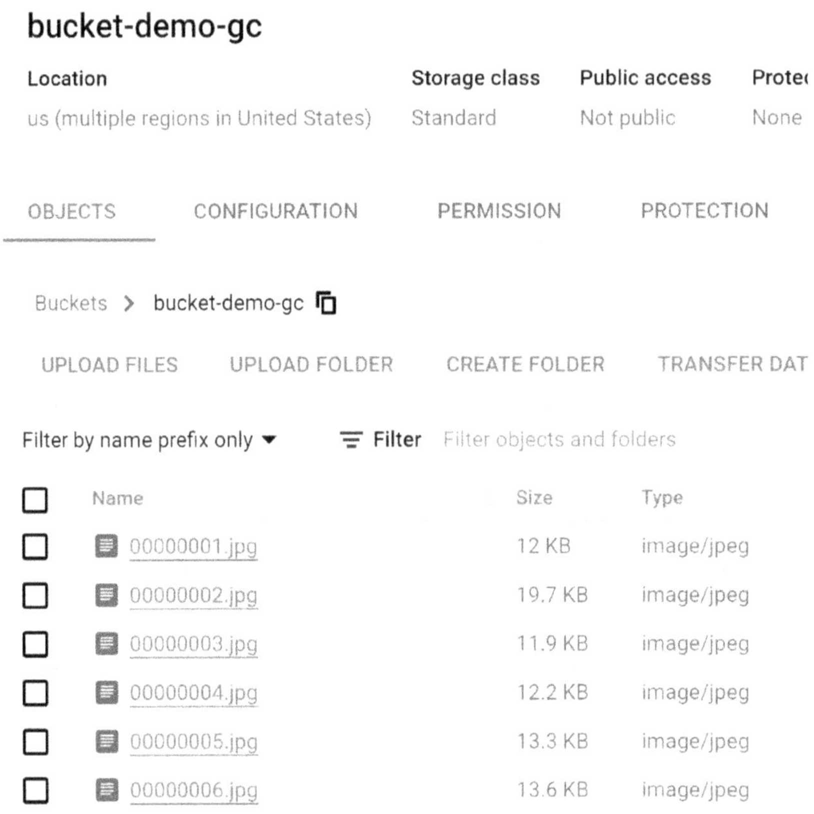

bucket-demo-gc

Location	Storage class	Public access	Prote
us (multiple regions in United States)	Standard	Not public	None

OBJECTS   CONFIGURATION   PERMISSION   PROTECTION

Buckets > bucket-demo-gc 🗐

UPLOAD FILES   UPLOAD FOLDER   CREATE FOLDER   TRANSFER DAT

Filter by name prefix only ▼   ⯐ **Filter**   Filter objects and folders

	Name	Size	Type
☐	📄 00000001.jpg	12 KB	image/jpeg
☐	📄 00000002.jpg	19.7 KB	image/jpeg
☐	📄 00000003.jpg	11.9 KB	image/jpeg
☐	📄 00000004.jpg	12.2 KB	image/jpeg
☐	📄 00000005.jpg	13.3 KB	image/jpeg
☐	📄 00000006.jpg	13.6 KB	image/jpeg

Figure 7.10: The Cloud Storage Bucket page with its objects listed

4. Head over to the BigQuery console by searching for it in the Google Cloud console and enable the APIs as required (it is pretty self-explanatory with the console prompts).

5. Create a dataset by clicking the three dots next to your project name and click **Create data set**.

6. Provide your **Data set ID**, **Location type**, and other details, and click **CREATE DATA SET**:

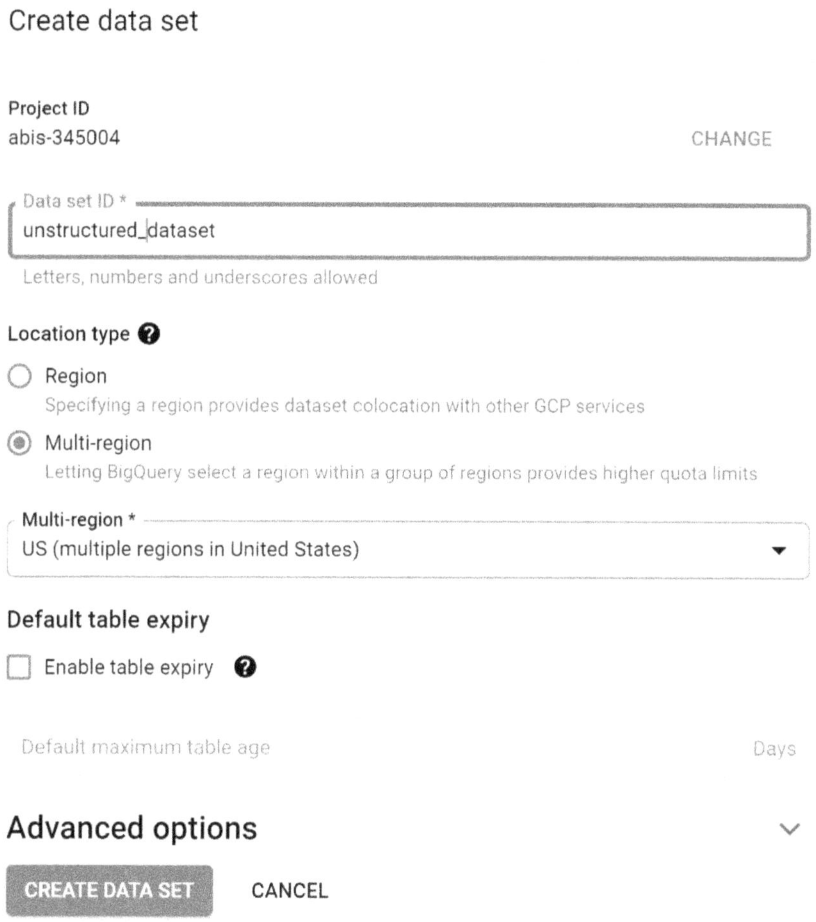

Create data set

Project ID
abis-345004   CHANGE

Data set ID *
unstructured_dataset

Letters, numbers and underscores allowed

Location type ❷

○ Region
   Specifying a region provides dataset colocation with other GCP services

⦿ Multi-region
   Letting BigQuery select a region within a group of regions provides higher quota limits

Multi-region *
US (multiple regions in United States)   ▼

Default table expiry

☐ Enable table expiry ❷

Default maximum table age   Days

Advanced options   ⌄

[CREATE DATA SET]   CANCEL

Figure 7.11: BigQuery's Create data set page

7. Remember the external connection steps we discussed in the previous section? Make sure your dataset and the external connection are in the same region.

8. A service account ID will be created as part of the external connection. You have to grant the necessary permissions to this service account to be able to access the images stored in Cloud Storage. You can do so using the following Cloud Shell commands:

```
export sa=<<"SERVICE_ACCOUNT">>
gsutil iam ch serviceAccount:$sa:objectViewer "gs://bucket-
demo-gc"
```

9. Remember the Cloud Storage bucket gsutil URI you noted? Copy that for the query in the next step.

10. You can create the object table using the following query:

```
CREATE OR REPLACE EXTERNAL TABLE `unstructured_dataset.test_
table`
WITH CONNECTION `us.unstructured-data-conn`
OPTIONS(
object_metadata="SIMPLE", uris=["gs://bucket-demo-gc/*.jpg"]);
```

11. This creates the object table and the references to the unstructured objects (images) stored in Cloud Storage buckets, as shown here:

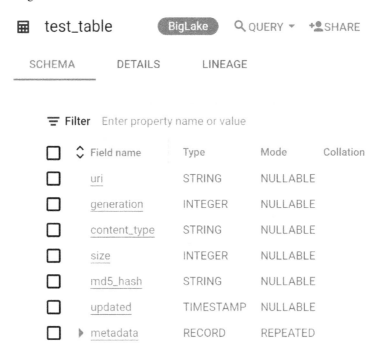

Figure 7.12: BigQuery object table schema

12. Use the following query to view the table's contents:

```
SELECT * FROM `unstructured_dataset.test_table` Limit 1;
```

You can validate the table's content with the query results, as shown here:

```
5   SELECT * FROM `unstructured_dataset.test_table` Limit 1;
```

Query results   ⬇ SAVE RESULT

JOB INFORMATION	RESULTS	JSON	EXECUTION DETAILS	EXECUTION GRAPH

Row	uri	generation	content_type	size
1	gs://bucket-demo-gc/0000000…	168355057…	image/jpeg	12292

Figure 7.13: The BigQuery SQL editor pane

Another way to visually interpret the result is to export the results that are displayed in the preceding screenshot to a CSV file. You should be able to upload the results to a CSV file by clicking on the **SAVE RESULT** option above the result set. Alternatively, you can query and extract results programmatically in your favorite programming language.

Are you intrigued yet about visually validating the result set stored in the CSV file? Let's try it out in a small Python code snippet so that we can view the data as an image.

Go to https://colab.research.google.com/ and open a new notebook by clicking **New Notebook** from the **File** menu. Copy and paste the following code into a cell, update <<your_csv>> with the CSV file extracted in the previous step, and run the cell's contents:

```
from IPython.display import display
from PIL import Image
import io
import pandas as pd
import base64
df = pd.read_csv('/content/sample_data/<<your_csv>>')
imgdata = base64.b64decode(str(df.data[0]))
image = Image.open(io.BytesIO(imgdata))
display(image)
```

This resulted in the Yoga Pose image I was querying from the object table:

Figure 7.14: Query result as an image using a Python code snippet executed from the Colab editor

If you have a structured data table, you can unify structured and unstructured data in a single query using a join query:

```
SELECT SPLIT(uri, "/")[OFFSET(ARRAY_LENGTH(SPLIT(uri, "/")) - 2)] as
pose,
a.health_benefit, breath, focus, data
```

The ability to unify structured and unstructured data with minimal effort and query them together gives organizations the power to derive impactful insights, which has been difficult to achieve traditionally.

Summary

Unstructured data has most certainly found its way through the heart and soul of every business these days. To take advantage of the data that is available to your business, irrespective of its size, format, structure, and source, you should ensure you have made the right design decisions for the storage service of your choice and the application that leverages it for your business. Keep in mind that the role of technology and platform providers when handling unstructured data should always be as follows:

- To enable businesses to get the most value out of their data by leveraging sources of all formats and types

- To manage and operate these services with efficient and automatic scaling, monitoring, encryption, security, and more, lifting the burden off of the shoulders of businesses

- To smoothly integrate across platforms, programming languages, and services, providing the business with diverse options to choose from while it's designing its applications

The unstructured data storage and processing services we chose to discuss in this chapter cater to the three crucial design expectations that I listed here.

This is where the use cases, hands-on guides, and exercises in this chapter will come in handy. If you have a use case with unstructured data in your application, try one of the services we discussed here. If you are a beginner at unstructured data hands-on usage, choose one from the list covered in the *Use cases* section of this chapter and try to implement a demo application for it.

In the upcoming chapter, we will discuss database operations, DevOps, and data modeling for advanced analytics.

Part 4:
DevOps and Databases

This part covers various design considerations, best practices, and tips for performance in DevOps. You will also learn about continuous integration and how it will help you in working with databases.

This part has the following chapters:

- *Chapter 8, DevOps and Databases*

8

DevOps and Databases

Just like with applications and other components of software engineering, databases also have a set of operational considerations and requirements. Starting from database setup, replication, backup, user access control configuration, monitoring, updates, patching, scalability, availability, resilience, disaster recovery, privacy, localization, performance, throughput, archival up to CI/CD, orchestration, and more, databases has its own laundry list of administrative demands. With the cloud, a vast majority of this list becomes automatic and fully managed by the service provider.

In this chapter, we will take a look at some of these attributes:

- Upgrades, updates, and patching
- Monitoring
- Security, privacy, and encryption
- Replication and availability
- Scalability
- Performance and throughput
- SLA, SLI, and SLO
- Data federation
- CI/CD
- Database migration service
- Systems, query, and performance insights

We will also discuss how Google Cloud simplifies the design decisions for these operational considerations.

Upgrades, updates, and patching

Upgrades, updates, and patching are essential for ensuring the security, performance, and availability of cloud databases. By keeping your databases up-to-date, you can help to prevent security vulnerabilities, performance degradation, and outages.

There are a number of different ways to manage upgrades, updates, and patching for cloud databases. Some of the most common methods include the following:

- **Automatic updates**: This means that the provider will automatically update your databases with the latest security patches and bug fixes. Google Cloud offers automatic updates for many of its databases. You can choose to have Google automatically update your databases on a schedule, or you can choose to be notified before updates are applied.

- **Manual updates**: If your cloud provider does not offer automatic updates, you will need to manually update your databases. This can be a time-consuming and complex process, but it gives you more control over the update process.

  If you do not want Google to automatically update your databases, you can manually update them. To do this, you will need to use the Google Cloud console or the `gcloud` command-line tool.

- **Third-party tools**: There are a number of third-party tools that can help you manage upgrades, updates, and patching for cloud databases. These tools can automate the update process and make it easier to keep your databases up-to-date.

- **Use the Google Cloud console or the gcloud command-line tool**: The Google Cloud console and the `gcloud` command-line tool are the most convenient ways to manage upgrades, updates, and patching for Google Cloud databases.

- **Create a plan**: Before you start any upgrades, updates, or patching, create a plan. This plan should include the following:

  - The types of updates that you need to perform

  - The order in which you need to perform the updates

  - The resources that you need to perform the updates

  - The steps that you need to take to recover from any problems that may occur during the update process

- **Test the updates**: Before you deploy any updates to your production databases, test them in a staging environment. This will help you to identify any potential problems with the updates before they impact your production databases.

- **Have a backup plan**: In the event that something goes wrong during an update, you should have a backup plan in place. This plan should include the steps that you need to take to restore your databases from a backup.

By following these tips, you can ensure that your cloud databases are always up-to-date and secure. The best method for managing upgrades, updates, and patching for cloud databases will vary depending on your specific needs. If you are not sure which method is right for you, consult with your cloud provider.

> **Note:**
>
> Please be advised that certain features and services described in the following sections may have undergone modifications since the time of drafting. The screenshots may look different from what you see in the book. APIs and versions may have been updated by the time you are reading this. As such, kindly exercise flexibility and adapt your steps accordingly.
>
> Additionally, some services may incur charges if they are outside the free tier (if applicable). Therefore, it is recommended to be aware of the services you are enabling and to delete or deactivate services and instances that are no longer required for learning or demonstration purposes.

Depending on your choice of cloud database, you will have different ways you can configure your database for auto upgrades and updates. In the case of Google Cloud's Cloud SQL, you can choose to do so from the Google Cloud console, on the Cloud SQL **CREATE INSTANCE** page under the **CUSTOMIZE YOUR INSTANCE** section, as shown in the following screenshot:

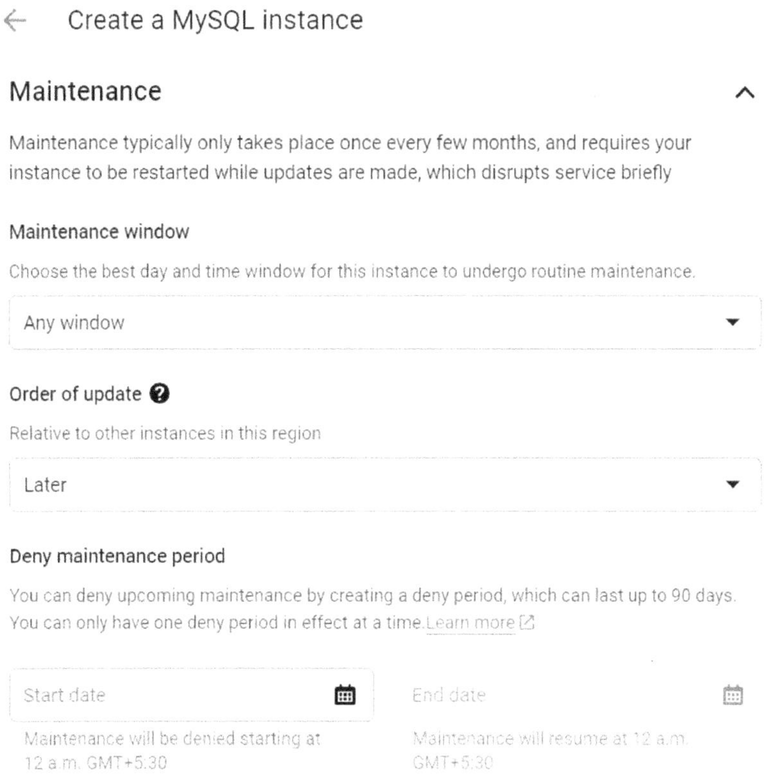

Figure 8.1 – Cloud SQL MySQL instance configuration

Let's discuss how we can monitor these databases.

Monitoring

Monitoring cloud databases is essential for ensuring their availability, performance, and security. There are a number of tools and services available to help you monitor your cloud databases. Some of the most popular tools include the following:

- **Cloud Monitoring**: Cloud Monitoring provides a comprehensive set of tools for collecting and analyzing data about Google Cloud resources, including databases. Cloud Monitoring can be used to track database performance, identify potential problems, and troubleshoot issues.

- **Cloud Logging (Stackdriver Logging)**: Cloud Logging provides a centralized logging service for Google Cloud Platform. Cloud Logging can be used to collect and analyze logs from cloud databases. This data can be used to identify potential problems, troubleshoot issues, and understand how users are interacting with databases.

- **Cloud Monitoring (Stackdriver Monitoring)**: Cloud Monitoring provides a centralized monitoring service for Google Cloud Platform. Cloud Monitoring can be used to collect and analyze metrics from cloud databases. This data can be used to track database performance, identify potential problems, and troubleshoot issues.

When choosing a monitoring tool, it is important to consider your specific needs. Some factors to consider include the size of your database, the type of database you are using, and your budget. Once you have chosen a monitoring tool, you need to configure it to collect the data you need. The data you collect will vary depending on your specific needs. However, some common metrics to collect include the following:

- **Database performance**: This includes metrics such as CPU usage, memory usage, and disk I/O

- **Database health**: This includes metrics such as database availability, database corruption, and database security

- **Database usage**: This includes metrics such as the number of database connections, the number of database queries, and the amount of data stored in the database

Once you have collected the data, you need to analyze it to identify potential problems. This may involve looking for trends, identifying outliers, and comparing the data to historical data. If you identify a potential problem, you need to take action to resolve it. This may involve adjusting the database configuration, upgrading the database software, or adding more database resources.

By monitoring your cloud databases, you can ensure that they are running smoothly and efficiently. This will help you avoid outages, performance degradation, and security vulnerabilities.

Let's look at it hands-on with monitoring for Cloud SQL. Go to the Google Cloud console and search for `Cloud Monitoring`, click **Dashboards** on the left pane, and select **Cloud SQL** from the list of dashboards that show up on the right. Pick the instance that you want to monitor from the inventory list. You should be able to see the metrics and details with visualization on the right pane, as shown in the following screenshot:

Figure 8.2 – Cloud SQL instance Monitoring dashboard

As you can see in *Figure 8.3*, you can choose from several other monitoring options such as integrations, services, metrics management, alerts, and uptime checks. It is interesting to note that with Google Cloud's Cloud Monitoring, you can monitor several services together by grouping the related services in the Groups section using the **CREATE GROUP** option. You can see a group that I have created for demo purposes in the following screenshot:

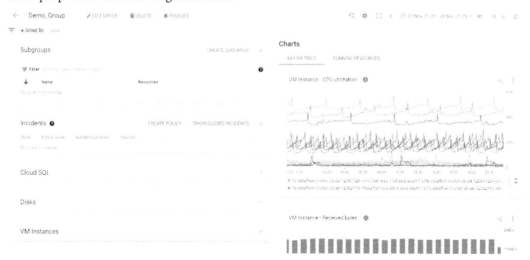

Figure 8.3 – Cloud Monitoring Groups page

Depending on your application requirements, choose the services that would make the most sense to be monitored as a group. It will come in handy when you want to understand whether there are other dependencies external to the service reflecting an issue while monitoring.

Security, privacy, and encryption

Security and privacy should be a major focus of any type of database design. There are some basic areas that need to be taken into account while choosing the design for databases:

- **Data breaches, loss, and corruption**: This includes design considerations to plan and assess your choices for data protection and back-up to prepare for factors such as hardware failure, software errors, human error, or natural disasters.

- **Data privacy**: This includes considerations to comply with data privacy regulations such as the **General Data Protection Regulation (GDPR)**.

- **Data security**: This includes ensuring your databases and data are secure and encrypted.

Here are some tips for mitigating cloud database security and privacy concerns:

- **Choose a reputable cloud provider**: When choosing a cloud provider, it is important to choose one that has a good reputation for security, and is a solution that encrypts your data and dependencies in transit and at rest.

- **Encrypt your data**: Encrypting your data at rest and in transit or making sure it is encrypted before it is stored in the cloud can help to protect it from unauthorized access.

- **Use strong passwords**: Use strong passwords for your cloud accounts and database access.

- **Monitor your cloud usage**: Monitor your cloud usage to detect any suspicious activity.

- **Back up your data**: Back up your data regularly to prevent data loss in case of potential data corruption or outages.

- **Stay up-to-date with security patches**: Install security patches for your cloud software as soon as they are available. Google Cloud services generally ensure these are in place for you unless configured otherwise.

Let's take a look at some of the features that Google Cloud databases offer to help protect your data:

- **Data encryption**: Google Cloud databases encrypt your data at rest and in transit.

- **Data isolation**: Google Cloud databases isolate your data from other users. This means that only you and your authorized users can access your data.

  This is done by using a variety of techniques, including the following:

  - **Project isolation**: Each Google Cloud project is isolated from other projects. This means that only users who have access to a specific project can access its data.

  - **Database isolation**: Each database within a project is isolated from other databases. This means that only users who have access to your specific database, table, and row (or specific object-level access) can access data.

- **Data auditing**: This allows you to track who has accessed your data and what they have done with it. You can use these logs to identify any unauthorized access to your data and to investigate any security incidents. Google Cloud databases provide detailed auditing logs.

- **Data compliance**: Google Cloud databases are compliant with a number of compliance and data privacy regulations such as the GDPR, ISO, SOC, HIPAA, FedRamp, HiTrust, and many such controls required globally and specifically to certain countries. This means that you can be confident that your data is protected in accordance with the law.

So far, we have seen some of the considerations for security, privacy, and other regulatory controls and how Google Cloud databases enable the security and protection of your data.

Replication and availability

Database replication is the process of copying data from one database to another. This can be done for a variety of reasons, including the following:

- **To improve performance**: By replicating data to multiple servers, you can distribute the load and improve performance

- **To improve availability**: By replicating data to multiple servers, you can ensure that your data is always available, even if one server fails

- **To improve disaster recovery**: By replicating data to multiple locations, you can protect your data from disasters

The primary reasons behind using data replication are to support high availability, disaster recovery, and to allow your data to scale without affecting the performance.

There are a number of different ways to replicate data for cloud databases depending on your need, some of them are listed as follows. The instance being replicated is referred to here as the primary instance and the replication copies are referred to as the read replicas:

- **Read replication**: This is primarily used for query and other application read purposes. It is the exact copy of the primary instance. It is used to process queries, read requests, and analyze traffic enabling load reduction on the primary instance. This could be created in the same region as the primary instance.

- **Cross-region replication**: This lets you create read replicas in a region different from the primary instance. The main advantage of this type could be that it allows for your data to be made available in a region that is closest to your application and provides disaster recovery capability for your data.

- **Cascading read replication**: This allows you to create a read replica under an already existing read replica in the same or a different region. The main advantage of this type of read replica is that it simulates the hierarchy of the main instance and its read replicas and the selected read replica could act as the new primary instance (with an exact similar hierarchy of read replicas) in case of an outage.

- **External replication**: External replication is the process of replicating data outside the network or platform of your primary instance. This could be a database hosted in a completely different network and platform setup, and the support for this type can vary depending on the configuration of the source and target networks and database platform providers. This type of replication can come in handy mainly in migration use cases.

Google Cloud databases offer a number of features that make database replication possible, including the following:

- **Globally distributed databases**: Google Cloud offers a number of databases for different formats, types, and structure of data that are globally distributed. This means that your data can be replicated to multiple regions around the world. This can help improve performance by distributing the load across multiple regions. It can also help improve availability by ensuring that your data is always available, even if one region is unavailable.

- **Automatic replication**: Google Cloud databases offer automatic replication for a number of databases. This means that you do not need to manually configure replication. This can save a lot of time and effort.

- **High availability**: Google Cloud databases are designed for high availability. This means that your data will be available even if one server fails. This is achieved through a number of features, including the following:

  - **Redundant hardware**: Google Cloud databases use redundant hardware to ensure that your data is always available.

  - **Automatic failover**: If one server fails, Google Cloud databases will automatically fail over to another server. This ensures that your data will always be available.

  - **Data replication**: Google Cloud databases replicate your data to multiple servers. This ensures that your data will be available even if one server fails.

In scenarios of disaster recovery, a replica can be promoted to become the primary in place of an instance that is going through an outage or corruption. Let's look at an example. In the case of Cloud SQL, if you want to set up a read replica, you can do so from Cloud SQL by choosing the instance and from the options available, selecting **Replicas**, entering the details, and clicking on **CREATE REPLICA**, as shown in the following screenshot:

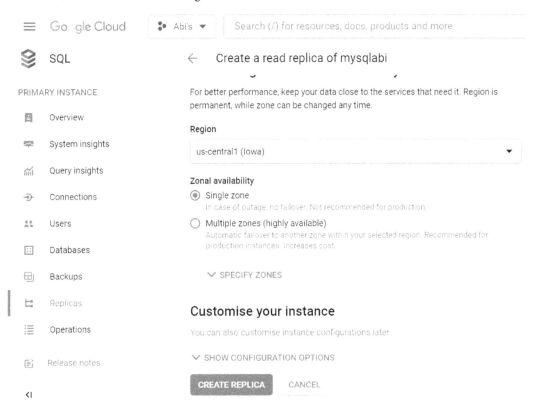

Figure 8.4 – The CREATE REPLICA page of a Cloud SQL MySQL instance

Let's look at how we can scale databases.

Scalability

Scalability is the ability of a system to handle increasing demands for resources. In the context of databases, scalability refers to the ability of a database to handle increasing demands for data storage and processing. There are two fundamental types of scalability that are vastly discussed:

- **Vertical scalability**: Vertical scalability is the ability of a system to handle increasing demands by increasing the capacity of its resources. For example, a database can be vertically scaled by increasing the amount of memory or storage available to it.

- **Horizontal scalability**: Horizontal scalability is the ability of a system to handle increasing demands by adding more nodes to the system. For example, a database can be horizontally scaled by adding more database servers to the cluster. Replication can also be considered as one of the ways of performing horizontal scaling, making the data more available within and across regions.

Simply put, horizontal scaling means adding more servers or machines to your resource pool, and vertical scaling means increasing the strength of your existing server or machine.

Google Cloud databases offer a number of features that support scalability, including the following:

- **Automatic scaling**: Google Cloud databases offer automatic scaling for a number of databases. This means that the database will automatically scale up or down in response to changes in demand. For example, if your database is suddenly receiving a lot of traffic, Google Cloud databases can be configured to automatically add more machines to the cluster to handle the load. If the traffic decreases, Google Cloud databases will automatically decrease the cluster by removing unused machines to save resources. These databases support horizontal and vertical auto-scaling. The type of scaling you would want Google Cloud to manage for you would depend on your data, application, security, operational, and cost requirements. The best way to address this would be to assess all of these considerations for your needs at design time.

- **Elastic pools**: Google Cloud databases offer elastic pools for a number of databases. This means that you can create a pool of database servers and then scale the pool up or down in response to changes in demand. For example, if you need to increase the capacity of your database, you can simply add more servers to the pool. If you need to decrease the capacity of your database, you can simply remove servers from the pool.

- **Sharding**: Google Cloud databases offer sharding for a number of databases. This means that the database can be divided into smaller pieces, called shards, which can be stored on different servers. This can help to improve performance and scalability. For example, if you have a large database with a lot of data, you can shard the database across multiple servers. This can help to improve performance by distributing the load across multiple servers. It can also help to improve scalability by making it easier to add more servers to the cluster.

In addition to the aforementioned features, Google Cloud databases also offer a number of other features that can help to improve the scalability of your database, including the following:

- **Geo-replication**: Google Cloud databases offer geo-replication for a number of databases. This means that your data can be replicated to multiple regions around the world if required. This can help improve availability by ensuring that your data is always available, even if one region is unavailable.

- **High availability**: Some Google Cloud databases offer availability as high as 99.999% SLA with zero downtime for maintenance.

- **Strong transactional consistency**: Google Cloud databases provide the most efficient and strict concurrency-control guarantees. This means the system behaves as if all transactions are handled sequentially even though they are scaled and replicated across instances for performance and availability.

  Read more about how these features are made available in the Google Cloud documentation: `https://cloud.google.com/spanner/docs/true-time-external-consistency`.

By using Google Cloud databases, you can easily and securely scale your database to meet the growing demands of your application.

Performance and throughput

Performance and throughput are two important factors to consider when choosing a cloud database. Performance refers to how quickly the database can respond to queries, while throughput refers to how much data the database can process per unit of time.

There are a number of factors that can affect the performance and throughput of a cloud database, including the following:

- **The type of database**: Different types of databases are suited for different workloads. For example, relational databases are well-suited for storing and querying structured data, while NoSQL databases are well-suited for storing and querying unstructured data.

- **The size of the database**: The larger the database, the more resources it will require and the slower it will be.

- **The number of users**: The more users that are accessing the database, the more resources it will require and the slower it will be.

- **The types of queries**: Different types of queries can require different amounts of resources. For example, simple queries that only require reading data will be less resource-intensive than complex queries that require reading and writing data.

Google Cloud databases offer a number of features that can help to improve the performance and throughput of your database such as automatic scaling, high availability, replication, external consistency, and so on.

There are a number of ways to measure the performance and throughput of cloud databases with Google Cloud. Some of the most common methods include the following:

- **Querying the database**: You can measure the performance of a cloud database by querying it with a variety of different queries. You can then measure the time it takes for the database to respond to each query.

- **Running benchmarks**: You can run benchmarks on a cloud database to measure its performance and throughput. There are a number of different benchmarks that you can run, including the following:

  - **Transaction Processing Performance Council - Benchmark C (TPC-C)**: The TPC-C benchmark is a commonly used benchmark for measuring the performance of **online transaction processing (OLTP)** systems

  - **Transaction Processing Performance Council - Benchmark H (TPC-H)**: The TPC-H benchmark is a commonly used benchmark for measuring the performance of **decision support systems (DSS)**

- **Using monitoring tools**: Google Cloud offers a number of monitoring tools that you can use to measure the performance and throughput of your cloud database. These tools can help you to track the performance of your database over time and identify any potential problems.

Once you have measured the performance and throughput of your cloud database, you can use this information to make decisions about how to improve its performance. For example, if you find that your database is not performing as well as you would like, you can increase the amount of memory or storage that is available to it. You can also try to optimize your queries to make them more efficient.

By measuring the performance and throughput of your cloud database, you can ensure that it is performing at its best and that it is able to meet the demands of your application.

SLA, SLI, and SLO

A **service-level agreement (SLA)** is a contract between a cloud provider and a customer that guarantees a certain level of service. For example, an SLA might guarantee that a database will be available 99.9% of the time.

Imagine you are the owner of a business that relies heavily on a cloud-based **customer relationship management (CRM)** system to manage interactions with your clients. You sign an SLA with your cloud service provider, and it guarantees that the CRM system will be available and accessible to your team 99.9% of the time over the course of a year. This means that you expect no more than 8 hours and 45 minutes of downtime in a year, ensuring that your business operations run smoothly.

A **service-level indicator** (**SLI**) is a metric that is used to measure the performance of a service. For example, an SLI for a database might be the average response time for queries.

Let's consider a video streaming platform. An SLI for such a platform could be the average video playback quality experienced by users. This metric measures factors such as buffering time and resolution. The SLI could state that the average video playback quality should be 720p or higher for at least 95% of the user sessions. This indicator helps the platform continuously monitor and improve the user experience.

A **service-level objective** (**SLO**) is a target value for an SLI. For example, an SLO for a database might be that the average response time for queries should be less than 100 milliseconds.

Imagine you are the owner of an e-commerce website, and you want to ensure a seamless shopping experience for your customers. You set an SLO for your website's load time, specifying that the average page load time should be less than 2 seconds for 90% of all user sessions. This SLO helps you maintain a fast and responsive website, reducing bounce rates and increasing customer satisfaction.

Google Cloud databases offer a number of SLAs, SLIs, and SLOs for different database services. For example, Google Cloud Spanner offers an SLA that guarantees that its globally distributed database service will be available 99.999% of the time. Cloud SQL offers an SLI that measures the average response time for queries. For Google Cloud Bigtable, an SLO could be defined as maintaining an average read latency of less than 10 milliseconds for 99% of all read operations. This SLO ensures that applications using Bigtable experience fast data retrieval.

Google Cloud databases are a reliable and scalable cloud database service that offers a number of SLAs, SLIs, and SLOs. By understanding these metrics, you can ensure that your database is meeting your business's operational requirements and user expectations.

By understanding SLAs, SLIs, and SLOs, you can make informed decisions about which cloud database service is right for your needs. You can also use SLAs, SLIs, and SLOs to track the performance of your cloud database and identify any potential problems.

Data federation

Data federation is a technique that allows you to query data from multiple sources as if it were all stored in a single database. This can be useful if you have data that is stored in different systems, or if you want to be able to query data from multiple sources without having to move it to a single database.

Federated queries are queries that are executed against multiple data sources. It can be used to join data from different sources or to perform complex queries that would be difficult or impossible to execute against a single data source.

Google Cloud databases support federated queries through the use of the BigQuery Federated Query Service. The BigQuery Federated Query Service allows you to query data from a variety of data sources, including the following:

- Google Cloud BigQuery

- Google Cloud Spanner

- Google Cloud SQL

- Amazon Redshift

- Microsoft Azure SQL Database

The BigQuery Federated Query Service is a powerful tool that can be used to query data from multiple sources. By using this service, you can simplify your data access and improve the performance of your queries. To use the BigQuery Federated Query Service, you first need to create a federated connection. A federated connection is a connection between BigQuery and a data source. Once you have created a federated connection, you can then use the BigQuery Federated Query Service to query data from the data source.

The performance of federated queries depends on a number of factors, including the size of the data sources, the complexity of the queries, and the network bandwidth between BigQuery and the data sources. Overall, by using this, you can simplify your data access and improve the performance of your queries. As a DevOps engineer or administrator, you would be really thrilled to be able to utilize such a capability for transactions and analytics that require data access across systems, databases, or source types.

Continuous integration/continuous delivery (CI/CD)

Continuous integration (**CI**) and **continuous delivery** (**CD**) are two important software development practices that can help to improve the quality and reliability of your software. CI involves automating the process of building, testing, and deploying your software. CD involves automating the process of delivering your software to production. By automating these processes, you can ensure that your software is always up-to-date and of the highest quality. You can also reduce the risk of errors and improve the speed of development.

CI/CD can help to simplify the management of cloud databases by automating the process of deploying database changes. This can help to ensure that database changes are made in a consistent and controlled manner and that they are tested before being deployed to production.

Google Cloud offers a number of CI/CD tools and services that can be used to automate the process of building, testing, and deploying software. These tools include the following:

- **Cloud Build**: Cloud Build is a service that can be used to automate the process of building and deploying your software. Cloud Build can be used to build and deploy your Google Cloud databases using a variety of languages and frameworks.

- **Cloud Code**: Cloud Code is a set of tools that can be used to develop and deploy applications on Google Cloud. Cloud Code includes a number of features that can help you to automate the process of building and deploying your Google Cloud databases.

- **Cloud Deploy**: Cloud Deploy is a service that can be used to automate the process of deploying your software to production. Cloud Deploy can be used to deploy your Google Cloud databases to production using a variety of deployment methods.

By using these tools and services, you can easily and efficiently implement CI/CD for your Google Cloud databases. They offer a number of benefits, including the following:

- **Scalability**: Cloud-based CI/CD platforms can easily scale to meet the needs of any project

- **Flexibility**: Cloud-based CI/CD platforms offer a variety of features and options that can be customized to meet the specific needs of any project

- **Cost-effectiveness**: Cloud-based CI/CD platforms can be a cost-effective way to automate the CI/CD process

When choosing a cloud-based CI/CD platform, it is important to consider the specific needs of your project. Some factors to consider include the following:

- **The size and complexity of your project**: If you have a large or complex project, you will need a cloud-based CI/CD platform that can scale to meet your needs.

- **The features and options that you need**: Different cloud-based CI/CD platforms offer different features and options. Make sure to choose a platform that has the features and options that you need.

- **The cost**: Cloud-based CI/CD platforms can vary in price. Make sure to choose a platform that fits your budget.

You might be wondering what kind of code and deployment you will be doing when you are managing cloud databases. Some examples are as follows:

- **Writing queries/code**: You will need to write queries or code to access the data in your Google Cloud database. These can be written in a variety of languages, including SQL, Python, and Java.

- **Creating and managing users**: You will need to create and manage users for your Google Cloud database. This includes creating user accounts, assigning permissions, and managing passwords.

- **Backing up and restoring data**: You will need to back up your data regularly in case of a disaster. You can use Google Cloud's backup and restore services to automate this process.

- **Monitoring your database**: You will need to monitor your database to ensure that it is performing as expected. You can use Google Cloud's monitoring tools to track performance metrics such as CPU usage, memory usage, and disk space usage.

Once you have chosen a cloud-based CI/CD platform, you can start automating the CI/CD process for your project. This will help you to improve the speed, quality, and reliability of your software and database deployments and services.

Migrating to cloud databases

Migrating databases to the cloud has become a pivotal strategy for organizations across the globe. In an age defined by digital transformation, businesses must be agile, scalable, and resilient to remain competitive. Cloud database migration is the key to achieving these goals and ensuring the long-term success of your enterprise. With all its benefits and tangible impact on business outcomes, it's only natural that more and more organizations and businesses are moving to cloud databases and the tools or services that they use for enabling this migration come with a lot of responsibilities.

When considering a cloud database migration service or tool, there are several important considerations and requirements to ensure a successful transition. Here's a comprehensive list of factors to keep in mind:

- **Compatibility assessment**: The tool or service should provide a compatibility assessment to analyze the existing database and identify any potential issues or incompatibilities when migrating to the cloud platform.

- **Data migration support**: It should offer robust data migration capabilities, allowing the smooth transfer of data from on-premises databases to the cloud while ensuring data consistency and minimal downtime.

- **Schema and object migration**: The tool should support the migration of database schemas, tables, views, stored procedures, and other database objects to the cloud platform.

- **Downtime minimization**: Minimizing downtime is critical. Look for features that enable online migrations or provide options for scheduled maintenance during low-traffic periods.

- **Data validation and verification**: A reliable tool should include data validation and verification features to ensure the accuracy and integrity of the migrated data.

- **Transformation and mapping**: For complex migrations, the tool should support data transformation and mapping capabilities to convert data types and structures to match the target database.

- **Security and compliance**: Ensure that the tool complies with security standards and data privacy regulations. It should support data encryption during migration and provide robust access controls.

- **Scalability**: Consider whether the tool can handle migrations of varying sizes, from small databases to large enterprise-level databases, without performance degradation.

- **Cloud provider compatibility**: Make sure the tool is compatible with the specific cloud provider you plan to use.

- **Backup and restore capabilities**: Having the ability to back up your data before migration and quickly restore it in case of issues is crucial for risk management.

- **Monitoring and reporting**: Look for tools that offer real-time monitoring and reporting features, allowing you to track the progress of the migration and address any issues promptly.

- **Cost estimation**: The tool should provide cost estimation features to help you understand the potential expenses associated with the migration process.

- **Version control and rollback**: It should support version control and rollback options to revert to a previous state in case of unexpected issues during migration.

- **Documentation and training**: Ensure that the tool or service offers comprehensive documentation and training resources to help your team use it effectively.

- **Support and maintenance**: Check for available support channels and the vendor's reputation for providing timely assistance in case of technical problems or questions.

- **Testing environment**: Consider tools that provide a testing or staging environment to validate the migration process and identify potential issues before performing the actual migration.

- **Customization**: Look for flexibility in configuring migration settings to accommodate the unique requirements and constraints of your database environment.

- **Post-migration optimization**: Some tools may offer features to help optimize the performance of the migrated database in the cloud such as auto-scaling and indexing recommendations.

- **Ecosystem integration**: The tool should integrate with your existing ecosystem, including data analytics and visualization tools, to ensure a smooth transition.

- **Long-term strategy**: Consider the long-term strategy and scalability of the tool or service to accommodate future database migrations and evolving cloud requirements.

Selecting the right cloud database migration service or tool is a critical decision, and it's important to align your choice with your organization's specific needs and goals. Thoroughly evaluating these considerations will help ensure a successful and efficient database migration to the cloud.

In the case of Google Cloud, there are different tools and open source services you can use to migrate to different Google Cloud databases. For example, migration to Cloud SQL can be done using **Database Migration Service**. Migration to Cloud Spanner can be done using the **Spanner migration tool**. These services are designed to cover some of the important responsibilities expected of the services you consider using for migration assistance to cloud databases.

Database Migration Service

In this section, we'll take a quick walkthrough of the steps involved in migrating a sample MySQL database to Cloud SQL for a MySQL database instance using Database Migration Service. We won't go through the full implementation/testing phase of the migration. We will just look at an overview of the configuration steps:

1. Go to the Google Cloud console and make sure your project is selected, or select or create your project, as shown in the instructions here: `https://cloud.google.com/resource-manager/docs/creating-managing-projects`.

2. In the search bar of the console, search for `Database Migration Service`.

3. Enable the API if you are prompted to, as shown in the following screenshot:

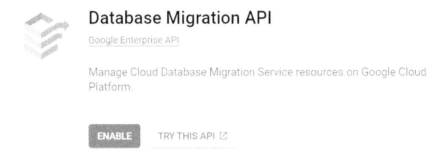

Figure 8.5 – Database Migration API ENABLE screen

4. Go to the IAM page at `https://console.cloud.google.com/iam-admin/iam` and make sure your user account has the **Database Migration admin** role assigned to it, as shown in the following screenshot:

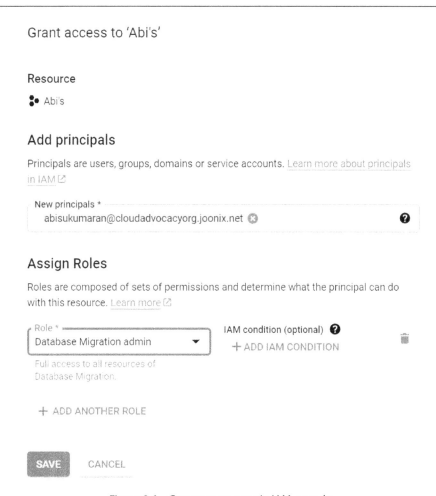

Figure 8.6 – Grant access page in IAM console

5. The source database can be on-premises or in a cloud provider. We'll assume that you are using a standalone MySQL database. You need to select this as the source database engine and **IP allowlist** as the networking method.

6. Next, we need to create a connection profile that contains the information required to connect to the source database and migrate to Cloud SQL. Click **CREATE PROFILE** on the page at the following link: `https://console.cloud.google.com/dbmigration/ connection-profiles`.

7. Enter the source MySQL connection details on the page and click **CREATE**, as shown in the following screenshot:

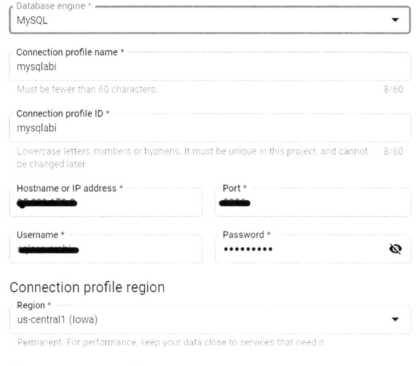

←   Create a connection profile

Figure 8.7 – Create a connection profile screen

8. Once the source connection profile is created, you should be able to see the list of connection profiles in the **Connection profiles** dashboard.

9. Create a migration job that allows you to migrate data from your source database to your destination Cloud SQL instance. Go to the **Migration Jobs** tab and click **CREATE MIGRATION JOB**.

10. Enter the details for the migration job in the migration job configuration page, as shown in the following screenshot:

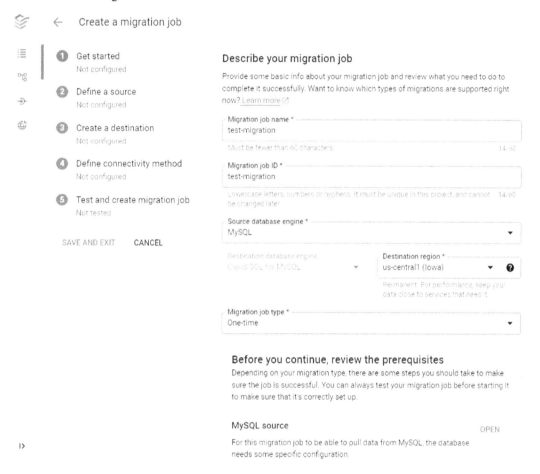

Figure 8.8 – Create a migration job screen

As shown in the screenshot, enter the **Migration job name**, select the **Source database engine**, and set the **Migration job type**. If you want the source database's ongoing changes to be migrated to the destination Cloud SQL database, set the **Migration job type** to **Continuous** instead.

11. Define your source and create your destination database instance, as shown in the following screenshot:

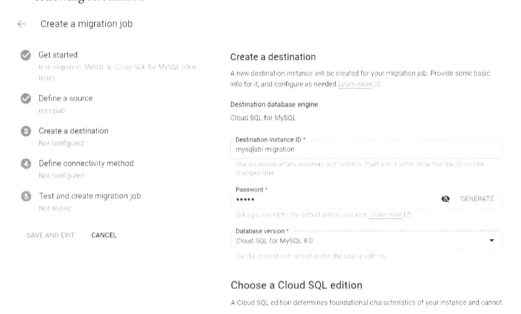

Figure 8.9 – Create a destination screen

Provide the necessary configuration details and click on **CREATE AND CONTINUE**.

12. Define the connectivity method, as shown in the following screenshot:

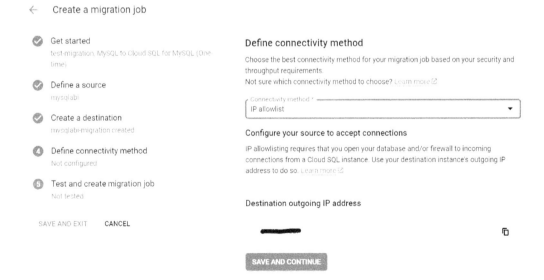

Figure 8.10 – Define connectivity method screen

In this case, I have chosen **IP allowlist** as the connectivity method. You can use this method to collect IP addresses to allow access to your data. Once the details are entered, click on **SAVE AND CONTINUE**.

13. Once all the preceding steps are complete, test and create the migration job.

We have only gone through the configuration steps for Database Migration Service. As an assignment for this chapter, try this out on your sample database and verify the migration results. To learn about these steps in more detail, refer to `https://cloud.google.com/database-migration/docs/mysql/quickstart`.

System, query, and performance insights

Understanding the functioning of your database system, application, performance, cost, and security-related factors are key considerations when it comes to database operations and observability. Google Cloud provides insights on system, query, performance, cost, security, and so on. System insights allow you to track important attributes such as system usage, availability, CPU utilization, disk utilization, database load, and so on, and proactively focus on finding patterns and taking actions. Query insights provide help in the detection and diagnosis of issues in the performance of your instance by examining queries in your application. There are more such insights. These insights provide information using historical and near real-time data, and at the same time, provide actionable prescriptive alerts with regard to your services. If you can enable these for your data and application, where available, you will be able to enhance the performance, availability, and quality of your databases, data, and application.

Summary

As for any DevOps team's dreams, the goal of this chapter has been to help you get started with understanding the fundamentals and importance of enabling organizations and teams to just focus on the business priorities and code, and leave the rest to the cloud platform. This way, DevOps teams can focus on more innovative activities that enable business growth while the platform keeps the lights on for you.

In this chapter, we have comprehensively explored the crucial intersection of DevOps practices and database operations with focused information on managing databases in the Google Cloud ecosystem. We have covered operational aspects such as maintenance, monitoring, security, privacy, encryption, replication, availability, consistency, scalability, performance, throughput, SLA, SLI, SLO, data federation, CI/ CD, migration, insights, and how to address some of these with Google Cloud databases and services.

In the upcoming chapters, we will look at data modeling and design considerations for AI/ML and advanced analytics applications.

Part 5:
Data to AI

This part will teach you how to design the best database that is optimized for various end-user tasks like analytics, ML, and more. You will learn to create collections focused on the needs of the customer. You will also learn how to utilize LLM applications for traditional applications.

This part has the following chapters:

- *Chapter 9, Data to AI – Modeling Your Databases for Analytics and ML*
- *Chapter 10, Looking Ahead - Designing for LLM Applications*

9

Data to AI – Modeling Your Databases for Analytics and ML

Businesses rely on analytics to gain valuable insights and make informed decisions. Cloud databases have emerged as a powerful platform for storing and analyzing large volumes of data. To leverage the full potential of cloud databases for analytics, effective data modeling is crucial. It involves a deep focus on the needs of data analysts, business intelligence, and data operations teams. It involves designing a database that is optimized for data analysis, such as querying, reporting, and visualization, and by extension for advanced analytics, such as **machine learning** (**ML**) and **artificial intelligence** (**AI**). In this chapter, we'll explore some key considerations and best practices for data modeling for analytics, ML and AI in cloud databases.

In this chapter, we'll cover the following topics:

- Modeling considerations for analytics, AI, and ML
- Data to AI
- Google Cloud ETL services
- Google Cloud Dataflow at a glance
- Real-world use cases for Google Cloud Dataflow
- Step-by-step guide to Google Cloud Dataflow
- Taking your data to AI

Modeling considerations for analytics, AI, and ML

As with relational transactional applications, analytics applications require data to be modeled, stored, and accessed to address the application's design aspects. While the business, functional, technical, and regulatory requirements vary for each application, there are some fundamental operational and design needs that are generally considered the baseline for all analytical data modeling. We'll look at a few of them in this section:

- **Understand the analytical requirements**: Before diving into data modeling, it's important to have a clear understanding of your analytical requirements. Define the specific questions you want to answer or the insights you want to derive from your data. This understanding will guide your data modeling efforts and help you design a database structure that aligns with your analytical goals.

- **Denormalize your data**: Normalization is a widely adopted practice in traditional database design to eliminate redundancy and ensure data consistency. However, in the context of analytics, denormalization is often preferred. Denormalization involves combining related data into a single table or document and optimizing query performance by reducing joins. Consider denormalizing your data model strategically to enhance analytical query speed and efficiency.

- **Partition and index data**: Partitioning and indexing are essential techniques for improving query performance in cloud databases. Partitioning involves dividing a large dataset into smaller, more manageable chunks based on a specific criterion (e.g., time-based partitioning). This enables parallel processing and faster querying of relevant data subsets. Indexing, on the other hand, creates data structures that facilitate quick data retrieval based on specific columns. Carefully select partitioning and indexing strategies based on your data access patterns and analytical requirements.

- **Choose the right data storage format**: Cloud databases offer various data storage formats, such as relational tables, document stores, or columnar databases. Consider the nature of your data and the types of analytical queries you'll be performing when selecting the appropriate storage format. For structured data, a relational database might be suitable, whereas unstructured or semi-structured data might be better suited for a document store or a NoSQL database. Assess your data characteristics and leverage the strengths of different storage formats to optimize your analytics workflow.

- **Leverage serverless and fully managed database services**: Cloud providers offer serverless and managed database services that eliminate the need for infrastructure management, allowing you to focus on data modeling and analytics. Services such as Google Cloud's BigQuery provide scalability, high availability, and automated backups for planet-scale data, simplifying the management of your database environment. Evaluate such services based on your specific requirements and choose the one that best aligns with your analytics needs.

- **Consider data governance and security**: Data modeling for analytics should also address data governance and security aspects. Define proper access controls, encryption mechanisms, and data retention policies to ensure compliance with industry regulations and protect sensitive information. Implement a robust data governance framework that includes data lineage, data quality checks, and audit trails. These measures not only safeguard your data but also promote trust and confidence in your analytics outputs.

Effective data modeling plays a critical role in optimizing analytics workflows in cloud databases. By understanding your analytical requirements, denormalizing data where necessary, leveraging partitioning and indexing techniques, choosing the right storage format, and considering data governance and security, you can build a robust data model that empowers your analytics initiatives in the cloud.

Now that we have discussed some of the most crucial design considerations for analytics data, let's dive deep into taking your data through advanced analytics.

Data to AI

This section is a perspective on data modeling for journeying from data to AI through several stages, including ingestion to storage, integration, transformation, and archival considerations:

1. **Data ingestion**: Data ingestion is the process of acquiring and importing data from various sources into an analytics database or data warehouse. When designing the data model for ingestion, consider the frequency and volume of data updates, data formats, and data integration requirements. Choose appropriate ingestion mechanisms such as batch processing, real-time streaming, or event-based ingestion based on the timeliness and velocity of your data. Ensure data validation and cleansing mechanisms are in place to maintain data quality during ingestion.

2. **Storage**: Choosing the right storage infrastructure is crucial for efficiently managing and accessing large volumes of data in AI workflows. Cloud object storage and database services such as Google Cloud Storage and BigQuery offer scalable options for storing structured, unstructured, and semi-structured data. Consider factors such as data durability, availability, retrieval latency, and cost when selecting the storage solution that aligns with your data modeling and AI requirements.

3. **Analytics database or warehouse**: The choice of an analytics database or data warehouse architecture is fundamental for AI analytics. Options such as traditional relational databases, columnar databases, and distributed data warehouses such as BigQuery provide different capabilities in terms of query performance, scalability, and cost. Consider the analytical requirements, data volume, concurrency, and budgetary constraints when selecting the appropriate database or warehouse architecture. Design the data model to optimize query performance, enable efficient data retrieval, and facilitate integration with AI frameworks or tools.

4. **Integration**: Integration involves consolidating data from multiple sources to create a unified view for AI analytics. Data integration can be achieved through **extract, transform, load** (ETL) processes, data pipelines, or data integration platforms. When modeling the data integration process, identify the relevant data sources, define data mappings, and establish data transformation rules to harmonize the data for AI modeling. Ensure compatibility between the data integration approach and the analytics database or warehouse to enable smooth data flow.

5. **Transformation**: Data transformation is a crucial step in preparing data for AI analytics. It involves cleaning, aggregating, and enriching the data to make it suitable for AI model training or analysis. Data transformation tasks may include filtering out irrelevant data, handling missing values, normalizing numerical values, or performing feature engineering. When designing the data model for transformation, consider the computational resources required, scalability, and automation capabilities to streamline the data preparation process.

6. **Archival considerations**: For long-term data retention and compliance purposes, archival considerations are essential. Not all data needs to reside in the analytics database or warehouse indefinitely. Define data retention policies based on regulatory requirements and business needs. Archive less frequently accessed or historical data to cost-effective storage options such as cold storage or tape backups. When modeling data archiving, ensure proper indexing or metadata management to facilitate future data retrieval if necessary.

By paying attention to these additional perspectives on your data modeling approach, you can establish a robust data pipeline that efficiently moves data from various sources to an analytics database or warehouse, ensuring optimal storage, integration, transformation, and archival processes. This sets the foundation for effective AI analytics, enabling organizations to extract valuable insights and derive maximum value from their data assets.

In the journey of taking data to AI, we have addressed storage and querying for transactions and analytics in previous chapters. In the upcoming sections, we will look at the ETL-related data modeling considerations with real-world use cases and Google Cloud services. So, instead of focusing on analytics queries, we will focus on the ETL pipeline services and components in detail.

Google Cloud ETL services

Google Cloud offers a comprehensive set of services to support ETL workflows, enabling organizations to efficiently process and transform data at scale. These services provide integration, scalability, and managed infrastructure for performing ETL tasks in the cloud. Here are some Google Cloud ETL services:

- **Google Cloud Dataflow**: Google Cloud Dataflow is a fully managed service for executing parallel data processing pipelines. It enables developers to build and execute batch or streaming ETL jobs using a unified programming model. Dataflow provides automatic scaling, fault tolerance, and data parallelism, allowing efficient processing of large datasets. It integrates with other Google Cloud services, such as BigQuery, Cloud Storage, and Pub/Sub, making it an ideal choice for ETL workflows.

- **Google Cloud Dataproc**: Google Cloud Dataproc is a managed Apache Hadoop and Apache Spark service. It offers a scalable and cost-effective environment for processing large datasets using familiar Hadoop or Spark APIs. Dataproc allows you to perform ETL tasks using Spark, leveraging its powerful data processing capabilities. It integrates with other Google Cloud services, such as BigQuery, Cloud Storage, and Pub/Sub, enabling smooth data ingestion and transformation.

- **Google Cloud Pub/Sub**: Google Cloud Pub/Sub is a messaging service that provides reliable, scalable, and asynchronous messaging between independent systems. Pub/Sub can be utilized in ETL workflows for decoupling data producers and consumers. It allows real-time data ingestion from various sources and enables smooth data flow between different stages of ETL pipelines.

- **Google Cloud BigQuery**: Google Cloud BigQuery is a fully managed, serverless data warehouse that offers high-performance analytics and SQL querying capabilities. BigQuery can be used as both a source and destination for ETL workflows. It supports data ingestion from various sources, including Cloud Storage, Cloud Pub/Sub, and Dataflow, and provides powerful transformation capabilities through SQL queries and **user-defined functions** (**UDFs**).

- **Google Cloud Storage**: Google Cloud Storage is a scalable object storage service that provides reliable and durable storage for unstructured data. It can be used as a source or intermediate storage location in ETL workflows. Cloud Storage allows efficient data ingestion and staging before performing transformation and loading processes. It easily integrates with other Google Cloud services, providing flexibility and reliability in ETL pipelines.

For your use cases and design, you can use some or all of these services to achieve your business requirements for performing analytics, AI, and ML on your data. In the following section, we will take a little more detailed dive into Google Cloud's Dataflow service.

Google Cloud Dataflow at a glance

Google Cloud Dataflow is a powerful and fully managed service for executing ETL pipelines. It allows developers to focus on data processing logic without worrying about infrastructure management. Dataflow offers a unified programming model based on Apache Beam, enabling consistent ETL development across batch and streaming data processing scenarios.

The key features of Google Cloud Dataflow are as follows:

- **Scalability**: Dataflow automatically scales resources based on the input data size and processing requirements. It can handle data processing tasks ranging from small to petabyte-scale datasets, ensuring efficient ETL operations without the need for manual resource provisioning.

- **Fault tolerance**: Dataflow ensures fault tolerance by automatically recovering from failures and providing reliable data processing. It divides the input data into small, parallelizable chunks and distributes them across multiple compute resources. In case of failures, Dataflow redistributes the failed workloads to healthy resources, ensuring data integrity and continuous processing.

- **Data parallelism**: Dataflow leverages data parallelism to process large volumes of data efficiently. It partitions the input data into manageable chunks and processes them in parallel across multiple worker nodes. This parallel execution improves the overall ETL performance and reduces the processing time for large datasets.

- **Integration with Google Cloud services**: Dataflow easily integrates with various Google Cloud services, including Google Cloud Storage, Google BigQuery, and Google Pub/Sub. This allows for easy data ingestion, transformation, and loading from and to these services as part of the ETL workflow. Dataflow also integrates with other data processing frameworks, enabling interoperability and flexibility in building data pipelines.

- **Unified programming model**: Dataflow adopts the Apache Beam programming model, which provides a unified API for developing both batch and streaming data processing pipelines. This unified model simplifies the development process, allowing developers to write code once and execute it in both batch and streaming modes. It provides flexibility and consistency in building ETL workflows for different data processing requirements.

- **Monitoring and visibility**: Dataflow offers comprehensive monitoring and visualization capabilities for ETL pipelines. It provides real-time insights into pipeline execution, including progress, data throughput, and resource utilization. Dataflow integrates with Google Cloud Monitoring and Logging, enabling the proactive monitoring, alerting, and troubleshooting of ETL jobs.

- **Managed service**: As a fully managed service, Dataflow handles infrastructure provisioning, scaling, and maintenance. This allows developers to focus on data processing logic and ETL pipeline development, without the burden of managing underlying infrastructure. Dataflow takes care of resource optimization and autoscaling, ensuring cost-effective and efficient data processing.

With these key features, it provides a very powerful and flexible platform for building scalable and reliable ETL pipelines.

Real-world use cases for Google Cloud Dataflow

You can use Dataflow to process and analyze data and systems in various real-world scenarios. I have categorized real-world use cases broadly in six areas, but this is not the limit given the capabilities of the Dataflow service:

- **Real-time data processing**: Google Cloud Dataflow is well suited for real-time data processing use cases. For example, a retail company can utilize Dataflow to process and analyze incoming sales data in real time, enabling them to track inventory levels, generate personalized recommendations, and trigger real-time notifications for out-of-stock items. Dataflow's ability to handle streaming data and its scalability make it ideal for real-time analytics scenarios.

- **Batch data processing**: Organizations can leverage Dataflow to transform and analyze large volumes of historical data. For instance, a financial institution can use Dataflow to process and aggregate transactional data from multiple sources, calculate metrics such as daily balances, and generate reports for regulatory compliance or risk analysis purposes.

- **ETL pipelines**: Companies can use Dataflow to extract data from various sources, perform transformations or enrichments, and load the processed data into target systems such as data warehouses or analytics platforms. This enables data consolidation, data cleansing, and data integration across different systems, facilitating comprehensive analysis and reporting.

- **IoT data processing**: With the proliferation of **Internet of Things** (**IoT**) devices, there is a growing need to process and analyze vast amounts of sensor data in real time. Dataflow can be employed to ingest, preprocess, and analyze IoT data streams, allowing organizations to gain valuable insights for predictive maintenance, anomaly detection, or optimization of IoT systems.

- **Clickstream analysis**: Web-based businesses often rely on clickstream data to understand user behavior, improve website performance, and enhance user experience. Dataflow can be utilized to process and analyze clickstream data in real time, enabling organizations to derive insights into user navigation patterns, perform sessionization, and deliver personalized content or recommendations.

- **Data warehousing**: Google Cloud Dataflow can be integrated with Google BigQuery, a powerful data warehousing solution. Dataflow can be used to perform ETL tasks to load data from various sources into BigQuery, apply transformations or aggregations, and optimize the data model for efficient querying. This combination of Dataflow and BigQuery allows organizations to build scalable and performant data warehousing solutions.

Leveraging these capabilities of Dataflow and other Google Cloud ETL services, organizations can derive valuable insights for business growth and decision-making.

In the next section, we will look at the setup, design, and implementation of the Google Cloud Dataflow service in the context of ETL in taking your data to advanced analytics and AI.

> **Note:**
>
> Please be advised that certain features and services described in the following sections may have undergone modifications since the time of drafting. The screenshots may look different from what you see in the book. APIs and versions may have been updated by the time you are reading this. As such, kindly exercise flexibility and adapt your steps accordingly.
>
> Additionally, some services may incur charges if they are outside the free tier (if applicable). Therefore, it is recommended to be aware of the services you are enabling and to delete or deactivate services and instances that are no longer required for learning or demonstration purposes.

Step-by-step guide to Google Cloud Dataflow

Let's get started with the steps involved in setting up Dataflow, creating a pipeline, deploying, testing, and monitoring a Dataflow pipeline. We will take a basic text processing use case for learning purposes and implement it in Java (my favorite programming language of all time – wait, what's yours?). The program reads any sample text you pass into it, tokenizes it into individual words, and counts the frequency of each word:

1. **Set up a Google Cloud Platform account**: If you don't already have one, sign up for a **Google Cloud Platform** (**GCP**) account at `https://console.cloud.google.com/`. Create a new project or select an existing project to work with. Make sure the billing is enabled for your project. You can follow the instructions here for creating new projects or selecting an existing one: `https://cloud.google.com/resource-manager/docs/creating-managing-projects`.

    All the following steps can be done with command shell commands or in the Google Cloud console.

2. **Enable the APIs**: Next, we need to enable a few APIs. To enable the required APIs in the GCP console, navigate to the project you've selected:

    A.   Go to the **APIs & Services** section.

    B.   Click on the **ENABLE APIS AND SERVICES** button as seen in *Figure 9.1*.

    C.   Enable the following APIs:

    • Dataflow API

    • Cloud Storage API (if you plan to use Cloud Storage for data input/output)

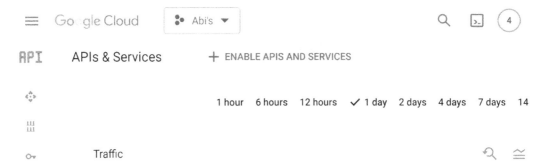

Figure 9.1: Enable APIs & Services from the Google Cloud console

The preceding figure shows where you can enable APIs and services in the Google Cloud console.

3. **Development environment**: To develop and run Dataflow pipelines, you can install and set up your own local development environment, if you prefer. This typically involves installing the necessary software and libraries.

Here are the general steps, if you prefer to set up a local IDE or use an existing one:

IV.   Install the **Java Development Kit (JDK)** if not already installed.

V.   Install the Apache Maven build tool.

VI.   Set up a code editor or **Integrated Development Environment (IDE)** of your choice.

If you use the Google Cloud Shell editor and terminal as your development environment (instead of setting up your own local IDE), you need not undergo the installation and setup steps. You can just click the **Activate Cloud Shell** icon, as shown in the following screenshot, to get started:

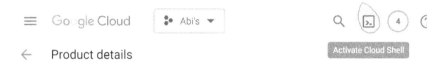

Figure 9.2: The Activate Cloud Shell button highlighted

When you click on the **Activate Cloud Shell** icon in the top-right corner of your Google Cloud console, you can open your Cloud Shell terminal, and from there you can navigate to the Cloud Shell editor.

4. **Create a Maven project**: In your preferred command-line tool or IDE that you just set up, create a new Maven project for your Dataflow application.

Note

A Maven project is a software project management and build automation tool used by beginners for its simplicity and standardized project structure, making it easier to manage dependencies and build processes in Java and other programming languages such as C# and Ruby, thanks to its flexibility and extensibility through plugins. Some popular alternatives to Maven are Gradle, Apache Ant, Apache Ivy, and Make. The choice of build tool depends on your specific project requirements, programming language, and personal preferences. Each tool has its strengths and weaknesses, so it's important to evaluate them based on your project's needs.

Use the following command to create a basic Maven project:

```
mvn archetype:generate "-DarchetypeGroupId=org.apache.beam"
"-DarchetypeArtifactId=beam-sdks-java-maven-archetypes-examples"
"-DarchetypeVersion=2.35.0" "-DgroupId=com.example.dataflow"
"-DartifactId=my-dataflow-project" "-Dversion=1.0"
```

As you can see in the preceding command, the initial project structure as defined in the `archetypeArtifactId` parameter is taken from the `beam-sdks-java-maven-archetypes-examples` archetype and so the basic functionality for the example projects will be already coded as part of this project. Execute the preceding command from Cloud Shell as shown in the following screenshot:

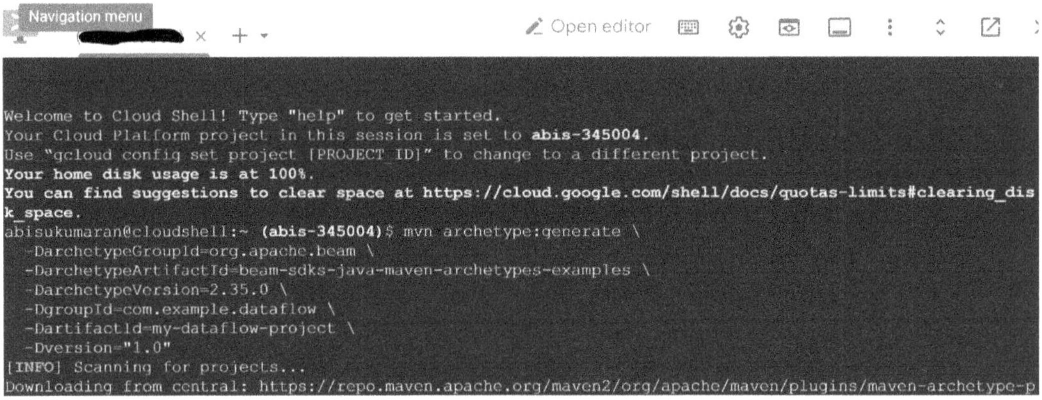

Figure 9.3: Cloud Shell terminal with the command to create a basic Maven project

This creates a project in your Cloud Shell machine.

It contains an example pipeline that we will look at here. We will run the example pipeline called `WordCount` present in the `my-dataflow-project/src/main/java/com/example/dataflow/WordCount.java` path. This class reads the sample text you pass to it, tokenizes it into words, and counts the frequency of each word.

5. **Define the Dataflow pipeline**: Inside your project's source directory, locate the generated Java file (such as `MyDataflowPipeline.java`) that contains the main pipeline code. In this example, you should see some basic boilerplate code in that file, prepopulated. Only if you want to add more functionality, modify the pipeline code to define your specific data processing logic using the Apache Beam programming model. This may involve reading data from a source (e.g., Pub/Sub or Cloud Storage), applying transformations, and writing the results to a sink (e.g., BigQuery or Cloud Storage). In our case, we won't change anything and use the example project that gets created as it is.

6. **Build and test the Dataflow pipeline locally**: Use Maven to build your Dataflow project. Run the following command in your project's root directory:

```
mvn clean compile
```

Run the preceding command from the Cloud Shell terminal inside your project's root directory. This compiles your code and resolves dependencies.

7. **Configure pipeline options**: You can configure various pipeline options such as the runner, input/output locations, and resource settings. This can be done using command-line arguments or by setting options programmatically in your pipeline code. Refer to the Dataflow documentation for more information on available pipeline options and their configurations.

8. **Deploy and run the Dataflow pipeline**: To deploy and run your Dataflow pipeline on Google Cloud, you need to create a Dataflow job. Execute the following command in your project's root directory:

```
mvn compile exec:java \
    -Pdataflow-runner compile exec:java \
    -Dexec.mainClass=com.example.dataflow.WordCount \
    -Dexec.args="--project=<YOUR_PROJECT_ID> \
    --stagingLocation=gs://<YOUR_BUCKET>/<YOUR_TEXT_FILE>\
    --output=gs://<YOUR_BUCKET>/output \
    --runner=DataflowRunner \
    --region=<YOUR_REGION> \
    --gcpTempLocation=gs://<YOUR_BUCKET>/temp"
```

Replace <YOUR_PROJECT_ID> with your GCP project ID, <YOUR_REGION> with the desired region for job execution, <YOUR_BUCKET> with the name of the Cloud Storage bucket to be used for staging and output data, and <YOUR_TEXT_FILE> with the text file you want to process with Dataflow. If the command throws errors (eg. Missing pom.xml etc.), try putting quotes around arguments (like for eg. "-Dexec.mainClass=com.example. dataflow.WordCount").

Once you run the command, you should be able to see the job running in your Dataflow console jobs list, as seen here:

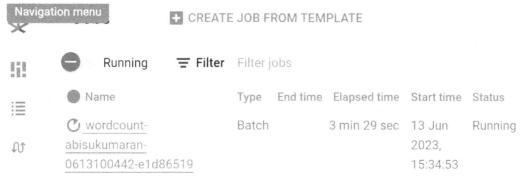

Figure 9.4: Jobs list in the Dataflow console

When you click the name of the job, you should be able to see the job graph, execution details, metrics, cost, and recommendations, as seen in the following figure:

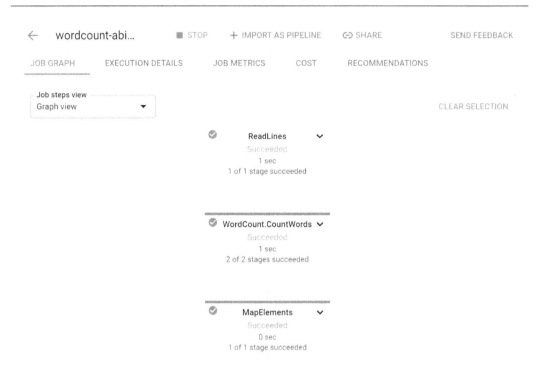

Figure 9.5: Job graph view

Once the job is completed, you should see its status as **Succeeded**. You can now validate the result file in your Cloud Storage bucket, which contains the tokenized words and the respective counts, as shown in the following figure:

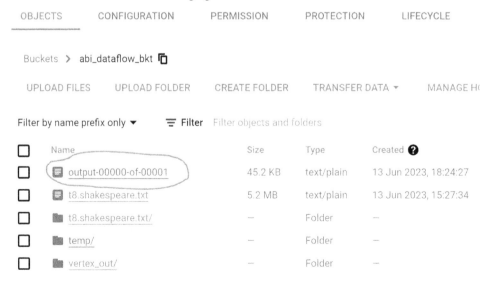

Figure 9.6: The Cloud Storage output bucket with its contents

Once you download the text file highlighted in the preceding figure, you can see the words and respective counts as seen in the following screenshot:

```
feature: 1
block: 1
Cried: 1
she: 48
sudden: 1
silly: 1
More: 6
out: 68
believe: 3
extreme: 1
Blanket: 1
unpublish: 1
ones: 3
duteous: 1
```

Figure 9.7: Text file from the output bucket

I hope you enjoyed getting started with creating your first Dataflow pipeline. Now you can move on to the operational aspects of the pipeline.

9. **Monitor and troubleshoot the Dataflow job**: After submitting the job, you can monitor its progress through the Dataflow monitoring interface or by using command-line tools such as the Cloud SDK's `gcloud` command. This allows you to track the job's status, progress, and resource utilization. In case of any issues or errors, you can refer to the logs and diagnostics information for troubleshooting.

That's it! You have successfully created a Google Cloud Dataflow project and deployed a Dataflow pipeline for processing data at scale. Remember to manage the life cycle of your Dataflow jobs, including starting, stopping, and updating them as needed. In this guideline, we provided a high-level overview of the steps involved in creating a Dataflow project. For more detailed information and specific use cases, refer to the official Google Cloud Dataflow documentation: `https://cloud.google.com/dataflow/docs`.

Taking your data to AI

Now that we have taken our data on a journey through a sample ETL pipeline, let's take it through one last step, which is to perform ML on the data output from the previous step, that is, tokenized words and their counts.

In this section, we will create a model to identify the context from the given list of words using word2vec and cosine similarity techniques. We will use the top 1,000 frequently occurring words (from the output of the previous step) to predict the context of the tokenized words generated from the pipeline we created in the previous section.

In this exercise, we will take the data we have generated through the pipeline as input data to the context prediction application we will build in Python. Don't worry, I have kept the code simple to understand and very minimal, so we don't spend hours explaining the steps and the code. Open a new Colab Notebook from `https://colab.research.google.com/`. Enter the code snippets in the following steps, one in each cell of your notebook and run each cell as you go:

1. Import the required dependencies.

    The dependencies included here will help us transform the text data in the file, convert them to vectors, and find similarities between words in order to create the context:

    ```
    import numpy as np
    import pandas as pd
    from spacy.lang.en.stop_words import STOP_WORDS as stopwords
    from sklearn.metrics.pairwise import cosine_similarity
    from gensim.models import Word2Vec
    ```

2. Open the text file that we obtained from the previous segment of this pipeline using Dataflow. Before you run this cell, make sure you rename the output file downloaded in step 8 of the previous section (Dataflow implementation steps) to "`t8.shakespeare.output.txt`". If you don't want to rename the file, remember to change the name of the file reference in the following snippet. Upload this output file into the current working directory (which is `/content/`). Alternatively you can write a few lines of code to read the file directly from Cloud Storage as mentioned in the documentation: `https://cloud.google.com/appengine/docs/legacy/standard/python/googlecloudstorageclient/read-write-to-cloud-storage#required_imports`:

    ```
    # opening the text file
    path = '/content/t8.shakespeare.output.txt'
    text = open(path).read().lower()
    print('length of the corpus is: :', len(text))

    word_text = []
    word_count = []

    with open(path,'r') as file:

        # reading each line
        for line in file:

            # reading each word
            for word in line.split():
    ```

```
                        # storing the words
                        if word.isnumeric():
                          word_count.append(word)
                        else:
                          word = word.replace(":","")
                          if word not in stopwords:
                            word_text.append(word)
                          else:
                            word_count.pop()

    print((word_text))
    print(len(word_count))

    word_count = [int(x) for x in word_count]
```

In this step, we open the file containing the text, eliminate the training : in the words, remove stop words from the text, and store the words and respective counts in separate lists. The last step also converts the word count to a numeric list.

3. Retain only the top 1,000 high-frequency words:

```
    df = pd.DataFrame()
    df['word_text'] = word_text
    df['word_count'] = word_count
    print(len(df))

    df = df.sort_values(by="word_count", ascending=False,
    kind="mergesort" )
    df = df.head(500)
    print(len(df))
```

In this step, we sort the word list by decreasing frequency and only retain the top 1,000 words in the DataFrame.

4. Create a word embeddings model.

    Here is a simple analogy that might help a 10-year-old understand word embeddings. Imagine you have a big book of synonyms. Each word in the book is listed with a list of other words that have similar meanings. This book is like a word embedding. It allows you to understand the meaning of words by looking at the other words that are related to them.

    In this step, we will create a word2vec model from the list we created in the previous step:

```
    wlist = []
    word_list = df["word_text"].values.tolist()
    wlist.append(word_list)
    # Load pre-trained word embeddings model
```

```
model = Word2Vec(sentences=wlist, vector_size=1, window=5, min_
count=1, workers=4)
model.save("word2vec.model")

embedding_model = Word2Vec.load("word2vec.model")
```

The `model = Word2Vec(sentences=wlist, vector_size=1, window=5, min_count=1, workers=4)` line of code creates a word2vec model from the `wlist` list. The model has the following parameters:

- `vector_size`: The `vector_size` parameter specifies the dimensionality of the word vectors. This is the number of features that will be used to represent each word. A higher `vector_size` will result in more accurate word representations, but it will also require more training data and computation time.

- `window`: The size of the context window. This is the number of words that will be considered when predicting a word.

- `min_count`: The minimum number of times a word must appear in the training data to be included in the model.

- `workers`: The number of worker threads to use for training the model.

The model will be trained using the skip-gram algorithm. The skip-gram algorithm predicts the surrounding words of a given word based on the context window. This allows the model to learn the meaning of words by looking at the words that are related to them.

Overall, the code initializes a word2vec model using the provided arguments and trains it on the given input corpus (`wlist`). The model will learn word embeddings with a dimensionality of one, considering a window of five words, and including all words that appear at least once in the corpus. The training will be performed using four worker threads for faster processing.

Once the model is trained, it can be used to do things such as find similar words, understand the meaning of sentences, and generate text.

5. Calculate the cosine similarity for the words.

   In this step, we will compute the average cosine similarity between a word and its surrounding words:

```
word_vectors = [embedding_model.wv[word] for word in word_list]
similarity_scores = []
for i, word_vector in enumerate(word_vectors):
    wv_list = []
    wv_list.append(word_vector)
    other_vectors = word_vectors[:i] + word_vectors[i+1:]
    for other_vector in other_vectors:
      ov_list = []
```

```
        ov_list.append(other_vector)
        #print(cosine_similarity(wv_list, ov_list))
        similarity_scores = cosine_similarity(wv_list, ov_list).
flatten()
        context_similarity = np.mean([similarity_scores])
    similarity_scores = np.append(similarity_scores, context_
similarity)
```

The average cosine similarity between each word and all the other words in the list in order to understand the meaning of words in context and to identify related words.

The snippet works on two main attributes:

- `word_list`: A list of words

- `embedding_model`: A word embedding model

It first creates a list of word vectors, one for each word in `word_list`. Then, for each word, the function calculates the average cosine similarity between the word and its surrounding words. The average cosine similarity is then appended to a list of similarity scores. Finally, the list of similarity scores is returned.

6. Extract the top words based on the similarity scores.

    In this step, we will extract the top-*k* words from the list based on their similarity scores to understand the meaning of words in context:

```
    top_k = 10

    # Get top-k words based on similarity scores
    context_indices = np.argsort(similarity_scores)[-top_k:]
    context = [word_list[index] for index in context_indices]

    # Display the extracted context
    print("Extracted context from the given word cloud:")
    print(context)
```

The preceding code snippet retrieves the top-*k* words with the highest similarity scores from the `similarity_scores` list. It then prints the extracted context, which consists of the words that have the highest similarity in the word cloud.

In this case, I used excerpts from the work *King Lear* by William Shakespeare, and the following figure shows the output with the context highlighted:

```
top_k = 10

# Get top-k words based on similarity scores
context_indices = np.argsort(similarity_scores)[-top_k:]
context = [word_list[index] for index in context_indices]

# Display the extracted context
print("Extracted context from the given word cloud:")
print(context)

Extracted context from the given word cloud:
['LEAR', 'I']
```

Figure 9.8: Code snippet displaying the context output

That is it! We have taken our raw data through a pipeline and implemented ML on it. As for the use case, we have used the Dataflow pipeline to transform the raw data to a word cloud and to store the result in a text format. We then used the words in that text file to extract the context from it.

Summary

Building upon the foundation of previous chapters, where we explored storage solutions for transactions and analytics, this chapter takes a deeper dive into data modeling considerations related to ETL processes and advanced analytics. Through the lens of real-world use cases, we examine how data modeling plays a crucial role in ensuring efficient ETL operations. Furthermore, we highlight the utilization of Google Cloud services as a means to address these considerations effectively with hands-on implementation.

At this point, having covered almost all the foundational aspects of designing for applications driven by data and databases of different types and structures, I look forward to engaging you with the most popular topic of discussion – generative AI. In particular, I would like to discuss the basics of generative AI and deep-dive into the world of **Large Language Models** (**LLMs**), covering the basics, design practices, and a hands-on implementation for extending your database application to perform LLM-based analytics.

10

Looking Ahead – Designing for LLM Applications

Imagine a digital solution that can comprehend, generate, and manipulate human language with great fluency and accuracy that has expanded the world of **natural language processing** (**NLP**) and **artificial intelligence** (**AI**): enter **large language models** (**LLMs**), where algorithms have evolved to transform the way we interact with systems utilizing the power of language.

So, what are these LLMs? An LLM is a type of AI model that can generate text, translate from and to languages, create different formats of content, and answer your questions informatively. It is trained on a massive amount of data, and it can learn the statistical relationships between words and phrases. This allows it to generate text that is similar to the text it was trained on. LLMs are still under development, but they have the potential to revolutionize the way we interact with computers.

In this final chapter, we will set the stage for data modeling for LLM applications by covering the following:

- The evolution, basics, and principles of LLMs
- The difference between data modeling for traditional analytical applications and LLMs
- Real-world use cases
- Data model design considerations for LLM applications
- Ethical and responsible practices
- Hands-on implementation to extend your database application so that it includes LLM insights

The main goal of this chapter is to equip you for the world of LLMs and their applications, aiming to help you prepare your data and design to handle the scaling use cases, challenges, and responsibilities.

Capturing the evolution of LLMs

LLMs are not mere algorithms; they are innovations, fueled by decades of research and breakthroughs. From their humble origins to today's awe-inspiring models, LLMs have surpassed expectations, with unparalleled computational power and vast datasets. They are gateways to a new era of language processing, enabling machines to comprehend, generate, and manipulate text like never before. LLMs have evolved but they started as early as the 1950s.

The following diagram takes us through a high-level journey regarding the evolution of LLMs:

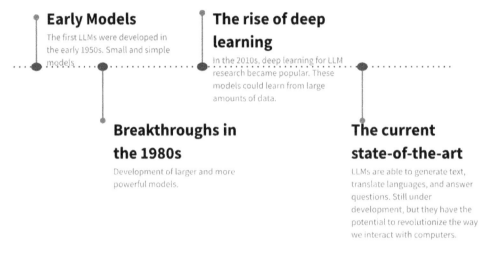

Figure 10.1: Evolution of LLMs

Some key research contributions have shaped the evolution of LLMs, such as the backpropagation algorithm (for training neural networks), the transformer architecture (for deriving context and meaning in sequential data), and the development of really large datasets. The evolution of LLMs is an ongoing process. As LLMs become more powerful, they will be able to perform more tasks and have a greater impact on our lives.

Now, let's understand data modeling for LLM applications.

Getting started with LLMs

Throughout this chapter, we will cover components and terminologies around LLMs and concepts that are crucial for data modeling for LLM-based applications. However, the detailed architecture involved in creating LLM-based applications is outside the scope of this chapter. Here is an overview of the architecture and functioning of LLMs, which are typically composed of three main components:

- **Encoder**: The encoder is responsible for converting the input text into a sequence of numbers. This is done by representing each word in the input text as a vector of numbers.

- **Decoder**: The decoder is responsible for generating the output text from the sequence of numbers. This is done by predicting the next word in the output text, given the previous words.

- **Transformer**: The transformer is a neural network that is used to train the encoder and decoder. It can learn long-range dependencies between words.

To give a high-level summary, LLMs work by learning the statistical relationships between words and phrases. This is done by training the encoder and decoder on a massive dataset of text. The encoder and decoder learn to represent words and phrases as vectors of numbers. The transformer then learns to predict the next word in a sentence, given the previous words.

Now that we have covered the foundational components of LLM, let's brush through some of the underlying principles.

Understanding the underlying principles of LLMs

Self-supervised learning is one of the underlying principles of LLM training. It is a type of **machine learning** (**ML**) where the model is trained on data that is not labeled. This means that the model is not given any explicit instructions on what the data means. Instead, the model learns to find patterns in the data on its own. LLM training relies on self-supervised learning, utilizing unlabeled data to predict missing portions of text and capture language patterns.

To give an overview, **labeled training** involves data with clear annotations or labels that's used to train ML models, while unlabeled training relies on data without explicit annotations, requiring models to extract patterns independently from the data. In other words, we can consider labeled training as similar to providing an answer key to an ML model, as it guides the model by explicitly indicating correct outcomes or classifications for specific data points. Unlabeled training is like handing an ML model a set of questions without any answers, requiring the model to figure out the responses on its own through patterns, associations, and contexts in the data.

LLMs excel at capturing such contextual information, assigning higher weights to words relevant to the context for generating coherent responses. Transformers utilize attention mechanisms to capture dependencies between words or tokens within a sequence. The self-attention mechanism allows the LLM to weigh the importance of each word based on its relevance to other words in the input. This attention-based approach enables LLMs to effectively model long-range dependencies and contextual relationships in text.

LLM training involves pretraining on unlabeled data to learn language properties, followed by fine-tuning specific tasks using labeled data. Language encoding and tokenization transform the text into numerical representations, enabling LLMs to process and understand textual information.

Let's consider the example of training an LLM for a text classification task, such as sentiment analysis:

1. **Pretraining on unlabeled data**: In this initial phase, the LLM is exposed to a massive corpus of unlabeled text from the internet. This data includes all sorts of text, from articles and books to social media posts and more. During this phase, the model learns to understand the fundamental structure of language, including grammar, syntax, and various contextual relationships between words.

   Example: The model encounters sentences such as "The weather today is amazing!" and "I can't believe how terrible the traffic is." It learns from these examples to recognize positive and negative sentiments, even though the data is unlabeled.

2. **Fine-tuning on labeled data**: After the pretraining phase, the model's general language understanding is quite advanced. However, to make it useful for specific tasks, such as sentiment analysis, it needs further training on labeled data. In this phase, the model is given a dataset where each example is labeled with the sentiment (positive, negative, or neutral).

   Example: The model is fed labeled data such as "I love this product; it's fantastic!" (labeled as positive), "This movie was a disappointment" (labeled as negative), and "The book was okay, nothing special" (labeled as neutral). Through exposure to many such labeled examples, the model refines its ability to predict sentiment based on the context of the text.

3. **Tokenization and encoding**: Throughout both training phases, the text undergoes tokenization and encoding. Tokenization involves breaking text into smaller units (tokens), such as words or subwords. Encoding converts these tokens into numerical representations that the model can work with.

   Example: The sentence "The weather today is amazing!" might be tokenized into ["The", "weather", "today", "is", "amazing", "!"], and each token is encoded as a unique numerical value. For instance, "amazing" might be represented as "Token 12345."

By the end of this process, the LLM becomes capable of taking a new, unlabeled text (for example, "I'm feeling great today!") and, based on its learned language properties and fine-tuning, accurately determining the sentiment (in this case, positive) of the text.

With that, we have demonstrated how LLMs can leverage both labeled and unlabeled data to understand and perform language tasks, in theory. Now, let's look at some real-world applications.

Comparing real-world applications of LLMs and traditional analytics

To understand the applications of LLMs in the real world, let's do a comparative study of the applications of LLMs with traditional analytics systems.

Here are some examples of traditional analytical applications:

- **Customer segmentation** is the process of dividing customers into groups based on their shared characteristics. This can be done to target marketing campaigns or to develop new products and services.

- **Risk assessment** is the process of identifying and assessing the potential risks to an organization. This can be done to develop mitigation strategies or to make informed decisions.

- **Fraud detection** is the process of identifying and preventing fraudulent transactions. This is implemented to protect users and reduce financial losses.

Now, let's discuss some real-world LLM-based applications:

- **Chatbots** are computer programs that can simulate conversations with humans. They are often used in customer service applications to answer questions and resolve issues.

- **Virtual assistants** are computer programs that can perform tasks on behalf of humans. They are often used to set alarms, make appointments, and control smart home devices.

- **Creative content generation** is the process of automatically generating text, code, and images. This can be used to create new products and services, improve the user experience, and generate new ideas.

As shown from the use cases in both scenarios, the main difference between how we would model our data for traditional analytics/ML applications and modeling data for LLM applications lies in the nature of the data and the tasks these applications perform. We'll discuss this in a bit more detail in the next section.

Understanding the differences in data modeling for traditional analytics and LLMs

Data modeling for traditional analytical applications focuses on creating models that can be used to understand and predict trends in data. This type of modeling typically involves creating tables and relationships between tables to represent the data in a way that is easy to understand and query. Data modeling for LLM-based applications, on the other hand, focuses on preparing data for applications that can be used to generate text, translate languages, answer questions, and create different kinds of content.

There are some key differences between data modeling for traditional analytical applications and data modeling for applications that utilize LLMs, as depicted in *Table 10.1*:

Considerations	Traditional Analytical Applications	LLM Applications
Data structure	In traditional analytics and ML, data is often well-defined. The data includes features and labels, and the modeling process focuses on learning patterns, correlations, and relationships within the data.	LLMs work with unstructured and natural language text data. LLMs are designed to understand language, context, and semantics in text, making them suitable for tasks involving human language understanding and generation.
Task specificity	Traditional analytics and ML models are typically task-specific. They are trained for a specific purpose, such as predicting customer churn, classifying images, or recommending products. Each model is tailored to a particular task and often requires feature engineering.	LLMs are versatile and adaptable. They can be fine-tuned for various natural language processing tasks, such as text classification, language translation, summarization, and more. Unlike task-specific models, LLMs excel at a wide range of language-related tasks without extensive feature engineering.
Training data and fine-tuning	These typically operate on a specific dataset tailored for the given problem domain.	LLMs require large-scale pre-training on vast amounts of text data from diverse sources. Fine-tuning with smaller labeled datasets adapts them to specific tasks.
Bias and fairness	They require some bias analysis, but the focus is often on data preprocessing and ensuring representative samples rather than language-specific biases.	Data modeling for LLM applications should address bias mitigation techniques to ensure fair and unbiased outcomes.
Language generation and creativity	These generally focus on extracting and presenting insights from data rather than generating new text.	LLMs generate text and exhibit creative language patterns. Hence, data modeling for LLM applications involves understanding and controlling the language generation process so that it aligns with specific objectives.

Considerations	Traditional Analytical Applications	LLM Applications
Computational requirements	These are relatively less demanding as compared to LLM-based applications, but this can depend on the use case and design considerations, such as the volume and variety of the dataset.	LLMs demand significant computational resources during training and inference. Data modeling for LLM applications needs to account for the computational infrastructure and scalability requirements.
Human interaction	Traditional models are often used behind the scenes for decision support or automation and may not directly interact with humans.	LLMs are designed for human interaction. They power chatbots, virtual assistants, and content generation systems, enabling direct engagement with users through natural language conversations.

Table 10.1: Differences between data modeling for traditional analytics and LLM applications

The choice between the two depends on the specific requirements and data characteristics of the application. By considering these key differences in data modeling for traditional analytical applications versus LLM-based applications, you can effectively design and optimize your data models to leverage the capabilities of LLM-based applications and cater to the specific requirements of natural language processing tasks.

Now that we have addressed a few real-world examples in both cases (data analytics and LLMs), let's provide an overview of some considerations of data modeling for real-world applications using LLMs.

Data model design considerations for applications that use LLMs

The best-suited data modeling techniques and principles for data model design for applications that use LLMs will vary depending on the specific application. However, some general considerations include (but are not limited to) the following:

- **The type of data that will be used**: The data modeling technique that is chosen will need to be able to represent the different types of data that will be used in the application.

- **The scalability of the app**: The data modeling technique that is chosen will need to be able to scale as the app grows. For example, if the app is expected to have a large number of users and growing attributes, then a NoSQL database may be a better choice than a relational database.

- **Data security and privacy**: The data modeling technique that is chosen will need to be able to protect the data from unauthorized access. For example, the data may need to be encrypted or stored in a secure location, may have privacy and regulatory requirements, and local laws preventing storage in specific formats and locations. Address data privacy and compliance requirements, especially if your application deals with sensitive or regulated data. Implement data anonymization, access controls, and auditing mechanisms to meet privacy and regulatory standards.

- **Data volume and velocity**: Consider the volume of data that the LLM application will handle. Large-scale language models often require significant computational resources and storage. Ensure your data modeling approach can accommodate the anticipated data volume and velocity, especially if the application generates or processes data in real time.

- **Real-time interaction and latency**: If your LLM application involves real-time interactions with users, prioritize low latency and responsiveness. Choose data modeling techniques that support efficient real-time data retrieval and processing to provide a smooth user experience.

- **Multimodal data integration**: If your LLM application involves processing both textual and non-textual data, such as images, audio, or video, consider how the data model will handle multimodal data integration. Some applications require combining structured information with other modalities, and your data model should support this seamlessly.

- **Versioning and data governance**: Implement version control and data governance practices within your data model design. LLM applications may evolve, and maintaining versioned datasets ensures reproducibility and tracking of changes. Additionally, consider data lineage and audit trails for compliance and accountability.

By considering such design questions and more, including the considerations addressed in the previous section, you can choose the relevant technique and principle of modeling that works best for the use case using LLMs. We'll discuss some of these in the next section.

Learning about data modeling principles and techniques

Data modeling techniques don't just help you with technology choices and frameworks – they also enable you to prepare the premises for the industry-specific use case that you are going to address with the dataset. Some data modeling techniques and principles can be effective in maximizing the potential of using LLMs in such applications while modeling the data for them:

- **Data quality and preprocessing**: Ensure data quality by performing rigorous preprocessing steps, including data cleaning, normalization, and deduplication. High-quality data improves the performance and reliability of LLMs and prevents them from learning spurious patterns.

- **Fine-tuning**: Leverage pre-trained LLMs as a starting point and fine-tune them on domain-specific or task-specific data. Fine-tuning allows the model to adapt and specialize for specific applications, reducing the need for extensive training from scratch.

- **Data augmentation**: Apply data augmentation techniques to increase the diversity and volume of training data. Techniques such as back-translation, word replacement, or paraphrasing can introduce variations and enrich the data that's used for LLM training.

- **Data abstraction**: This is the process of representing data in a way that is independent of the physical implementation of the data. Data abstraction is important for applications that use LLMs as it can help make the application more portable and scalable.

- **Data normalization**: This is the process of organizing data in a way that minimizes redundancy and ensures that data is consistent. Normalized data modeling may be preferable when data consistency, scalability, and long-term maintainability are critical considerations for the LLM-based analytics application. Denormalized data modeling can be suitable when the emphasis is on optimizing query performance, simplifying data access, and supporting LLM model training. Ultimately, the decision between denormalized and normalized data modeling depends on factors such as the nature of the data, the specific analytics requirements, the performance considerations, and the long-term scalability needs of the application. You need to carefully evaluate these factors and choose a data modeling approach that aligns with the objectives and constraints of your specific LLM-based analytics use case.

- **Domain-specific adaptation**: Incorporate domain-specific knowledge and adapt the data model accordingly. This involves curating domain-specific datasets, incorporating domain-specific features, and aligning the data model with the specific requirements of the target domain.

- **Bias detection and mitigation**: Develop techniques to detect and mitigate bias present in the data used for training. This can involve analyzing and addressing bias related to gender, race, or other sensitive attributes, promoting fairness and inclusivity in the application's outputs. Make sure that you eliminate bias from your data as part of this process so that you don't get skewed results for your models.

- **Data integrity**: This is the principle that data should be accurate, complete, and consistent. Data integrity is important for applications that use LLMs as it can help ensure that the results of the application are accurate and reliable.

- **Explainability and interpretability**: Use methods to explain and interpret the decisions made by LLMs. Techniques such as attention mechanisms (paying close attention to specific parts), saliency analysis (analyzing what stands out), model-agnostic approaches (general methods that work with any model), and more help us see how the model makes decisions, making it clearer and more trustworthy.

- **Continuous evaluation and feedback loop**: Establish mechanisms for continuous evaluation and feedback to iteratively improve the data model. Collect user feedback, monitor performance metrics, and incorporate insights into the data model's design to enhance its effectiveness over time.

- **Ethical and responsible data practices**: Embrace ethical considerations in data modeling, such as user privacy, data security, and fair data usage. Adhere to legal and regulatory requirements, promote transparency, and ensure responsible handling of sensitive information.

These are some of the top considerations, techniques, and principles to address when we are data modeling LLM-based applications.

Next, we will focus on ethical and responsible data practices.

Ethical and responsible practices

In today's world, where AI plays a pivotal role, it's crucial to incorporate ethical practices to ensure that businesses and developers use LLMs in a way that benefits society and minimizes harm. Ethics in AI involves making responsible and morally sound choices when developing and deploying AI systems. In this section, we will discuss some of the core ethical and responsible data model design considerations for applications that use LLMs:

- Ensure that data that's used for training LLMs is collected and stored following ethical and legal guidelines, respecting user privacy rights. Implement robust security measures to protect sensitive data from unauthorized access:

  - It is imperative to obtain informed consent from users when collecting their data, clearly stating how their information will be used. Transparency in data collection practices builds trust with users and safeguards their privacy.

  - Regularly update data handling and storage practices to comply with evolving privacy regulations. Privacy laws and regulations, such as the **General Data Protection Regulation** (**GDPR**) and the **California Consumer Privacy Act** (**CCPA**), are constantly evolving. Staying up-to-date and in compliance with these regulations is crucial to protect user privacy and avoid legal complications.

  - Consider adopting data anonymization techniques when handling personal data. Anonymizing user data means removing **personally identifiable information** (**PII**) to minimize the risk of data breaches or misuse. However, it's important to note that even anonymized data should be handled with care to prevent re-identification.

- Take proactive steps to identify and mitigate bias present in the training data. Carefully curate diverse and representative datasets to avoid perpetuating biased outcomes or discriminatory behavior in LLM applications.

  - Bias can unintentionally infiltrate AI models when training data reflects existing societal biases, such as gender, race, or socioeconomic disparities. This can lead to biased predictions and reinforce harmful stereotypes, undermining the fairness and credibility of AI applications. Hence, proactively identifying and mitigating biases is imperative to ensure equitable and ethical outcomes in LLM applications.

- Strive for transparency in LLM models by providing clear explanations of how they make predictions or generate responses. Develop methods to interpret and understand the reasoning behind LLM outputs, promoting accountability and trust.

  - Explainability in LLM models is crucial because it allows users and stakeholders to understand why a particular prediction or response was generated. This transparency fosters trust in AI systems and enables accountability in decision-making processes.

- Establish proper data governance frameworks and obtain informed consent when collecting or using data for LLM training. Respect user preferences regarding data usage, providing mechanisms for opt-in and opt-out to ensure transparency and control:

  - Data governance refers to the set of policies, procedures, and practices that organizations establish to manage their data effectively. It involves defining data ownership, roles, responsibilities, and data quality standards.

  - Various frameworks are available to help organizations implement robust data governance. Some widely recognized frameworks are **Control Objectives for Information and Related Technologies** (**COBIT**), **The Open Group Architecture Framework** (**TOGAF**), and ISO 27001. These frameworks offer structured methodologies and best practices for data governance, ensuring data is managed ethically and securely.

- Conduct periodic audits of applications using the models to assess their performance, behavior, and potential bias. Continuously monitor and evaluate the impact of LLM applications, making necessary adjustments so that you align with ethical standards.

- Deploy LLM applications responsibly, taking into account potential social, cultural, and ethical implications. Consider the potential risks and unintended consequences associated with widespread adoption, and actively work to address them.

- Empower users by providing clear information about how their data is being used and shared within LLM applications. Educate users about the capabilities and limitations of LLMs, enabling them to make informed decisions regarding their interactions with such applications.

- Encourage collaboration within the industry to establish standards and guidelines for ethical data modeling practices in LLM applications. Promote open dialogue, knowledge sharing, and responsible innovation to collectively address challenges and foster ethical practices.

- Regularly assess the ethical implications of data models and LLM applications as technology evolves. Stay updated on emerging ethical considerations and adapt data model designs accordingly to ensure the responsible and sustainable use of LLMs.

By following these ethical and responsible data model design practices, applications that utilize LLMs can strive to maximize their benefits while minimizing potential harms, fostering trust, fairness, and accountability in the development and deployment of LLM technologies.

Now that we have covered the basics and design considerations for enabling data so that we can build LLM applications, it's hands-on time!

Hands-on time – building an LLM application

All the databases we have discussed in this book so far support Generative AI in some form or the other. Either store, manage, and process the data that you end up using for your LLM application or provide remote methods and APIs that directly support LLMs on your data. There are also vector databases. I have explained these briefly toward the end of this chapter.

In this section, we will take a hands-on approach to creating an LLM application in BigQuery with **BigQuery Machine Learning** (**BQML**) only using SQL queries, directly on the data stored in a BigQuery table.

> **Note:**
>
> Please be advised that certain features and services described in the following sections may have undergone modifications since the time of drafting. The screenshots may look different from what you see in the book. APIs and versions may have been updated by the time you are reading this. As such, kindly exercise flexibility and adapt your steps accordingly.
>
> Additionally, some services may incur charges if they are outside the free tier (if applicable). Therefore, it is recommended to be aware of the services you are enabling and to delete or deactivate services and instances that are no longer required for learning or demonstration purposes.

Why did we choose BigQuery for this? While there are many reasons why BigQuery is the key to a lot of data design considerations, the answer here is simple and three-fold:

- LLM meets your data, where it lives!
- Since you are creating this only using SQL, it doesn't require programming expertise
- Since BigQuery supports storing and managing all data structures, you can unify your data with other formats of data, which could help in creating more precise analytics, ML, and LLM models

How are we going to implement this? We will use Google Cloud's generative AI APIs from Vertex AI as hosted remote functions in BigQuery to implement the LLM application.

The following is from the Google documentation:

- The generative AI APIs from Vertex AI lets you test, customize, and deploy instances of Google's LLMs so that you can leverage the generative AI capabilities in your applications. You can read more about it here: `https://cloud.google.com/vertex-ai/docs/generative-ai/start/quickstarts/api-quickstart`.
- You can register a Vertex AI endpoint as a remote model and call it directly from BigQuery with `ML.PREDICT` construct. You can read more about this here: `https://cloud.google.com/bigquery/docs/bigquery-ml-remote-model-tutorial`.

- We will use the CLOUD_AI_LARGE_LANGUAGE_MODEL_V1 (the name may be different when you are reading this. Please refer to the BigQuery documentation to make sure you are invoking the latest text generation API available as a remote service for BigQuery) remote service type from Vertex AI in this implementation.

What are we going to implement? We will build a text generation model that will read a word from a BigQuery table and generate a two-line explanation for it.

Prerequisites:

- This chapter assumes you've already created a Google Cloud project, enabled BigQuery, and created a BigQuery dataset. Since we covered these steps in detail in *Chapter 5, Designing an Analytical Data Warehouse*, in the *Setting up and configuring a fully managed data warehouse with BigQuery* section, I encourage you to follow the steps in that chapter.

- Before you begin, it is assumed that you have a dataset named bq_llm created.

- It's also assumed that you have all the necessary APIs enabled – that is, the BigQuery API, BigQuery Connection API, and Vertex AI API, as mentioned in the documentation at https://cloud.google.com/endpoints/docs/openapi/enable-api. This was also covered in some of the previous chapters of this book.

Step 1 – create a table

Let's create a table named words in the BigQuery dataset we just created – that is, bq_llm. In the BigQuery console's query editor pane, type the following command:

```
create table bq_llm.words(id integer, word string);
```

Click **RUN**, as shown here:

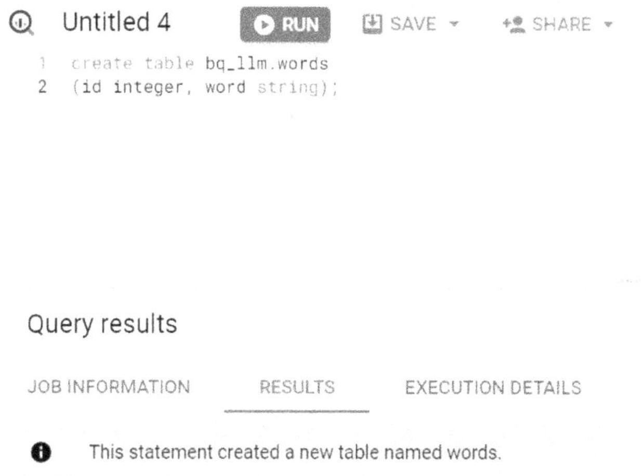

Figure 10.2: BigQuery SQL editor with the CREATE TABLE statement

As you can see, once you run the CREATE TABLE statement, you should be able to go to the **Query results** pane and see that the statement created a new table named words.

Step 2 – insert data into the table

Let's insert two rows into the words table we just created. Paste the following statements in the query editor:

```
insert into bq_llm.words values(1, 'LLM');
insert into bq_llm.words values(2, 'Generative AI');
insert into bq_llm.words values(3, 'Observability');
```

Click **RUN**:

Status	End time	SQL	Stages completed	Bytes processed	Action
✓	09:57 [1:1]	insert into bq_llm.words values(1, 'LLM')	3	0 B	**VIEW RESULTS**
✓	09:57 [2:1]	insert into bq_llm.words values(2, 'Gen...	3	0 B	**VIEW RESULTS**
✓	09:57 [3:1]	insert into bq_llm.words values(3, 'Obs...	3	0 B	**VIEW RESULTS**

Figure 10.3: BigQuery SQL editor with the INSERT statement

As you can see, once you run the INSERT statement, the three rows will be inserted into the words table.

Step 3 – create an external connection for BigQuery to access the Vertex AI model

Let's create an external connection and make a note of the Service Account ID from the connection configuration details. Make sure the BQ Connection API is enabled for this step to be successful. To do this, just search for `BigQuery connection API` in the search bar of Google Cloud Console and enable the API when you're prompted:

1. Click the + **ADD** button in the **Explorer** pane of BigQuery, as shown here:

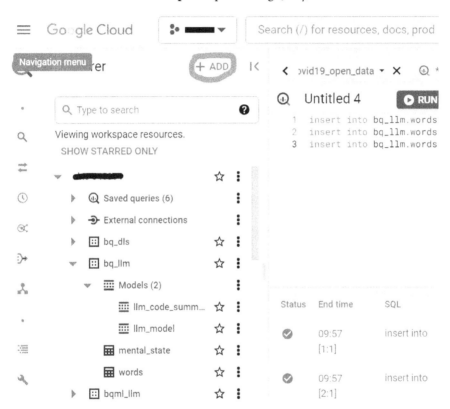

Figure 10.4: The BigQuery Explorer pane with the + ADD button highlighted

The preceding screenshot shows the + **ADD** button that you need to click to create the external connection.

2.   Once you click that, you should be able to see the **Add** page. Under **Popular sources**, choose **Connections to external data sources**, as shown here:

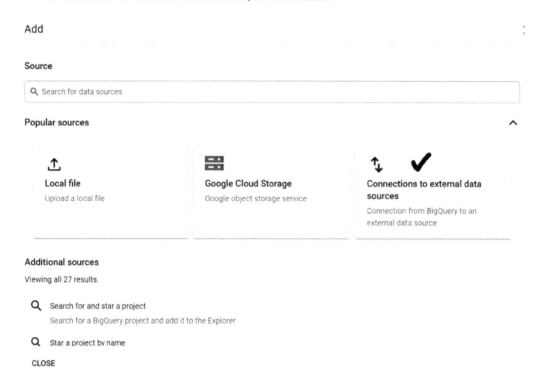

Figure 10.5: The Connections to external data sources option

Once you've done this, you will be taken to the **External data source** page, as shown here:

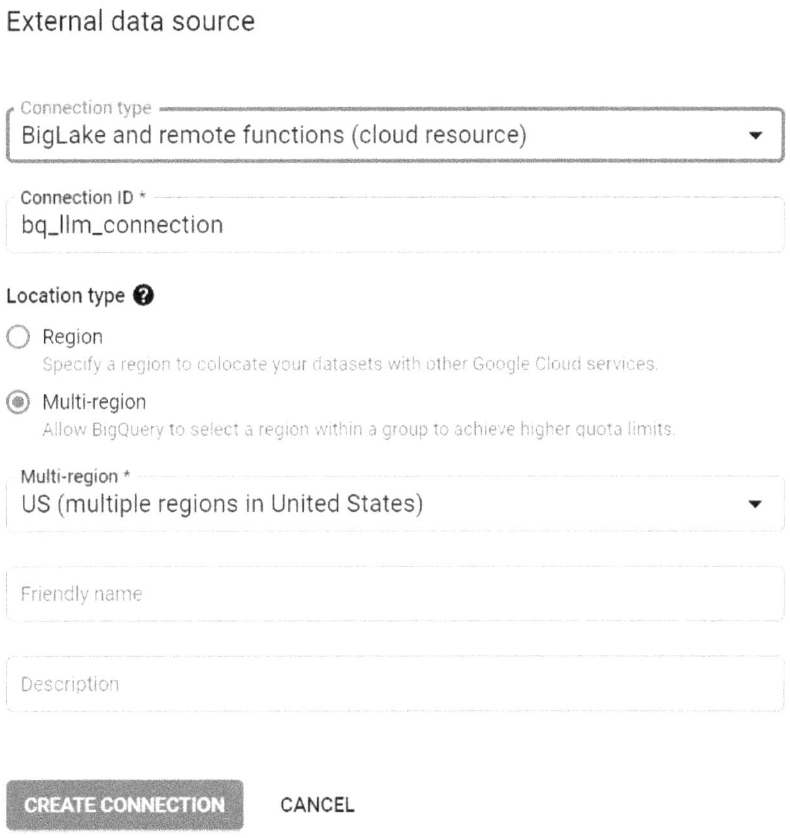

External data source

Connection type
BigLake and remote functions (cloud resource)   ▼

Connection ID *
bq_llm_connection

Location type ❓

◯ Region
   Specify a region to colocate your datasets with other Google Cloud services.

◉ Multi-region
   Allow BigQuery to select a region within a group to achieve higher quota limits.

Multi-region *
US (multiple regions in United States)   ▼

Friendly name

Description

[CREATE CONNECTION]   CANCEL

Figure 19.6: The External data source page

Enter the necessary details and click **CREATE CONNECTION**, as shown in the preceding screenshot. Make sure your connection type is set to **BigLake and remote functions (cloud resource)** and that **Location type** is the same as that of your BigQuery dataset.

3. Upon clicking **CREATE CONNECTION**, you will be taken to the **Connection info** page, as shown here:

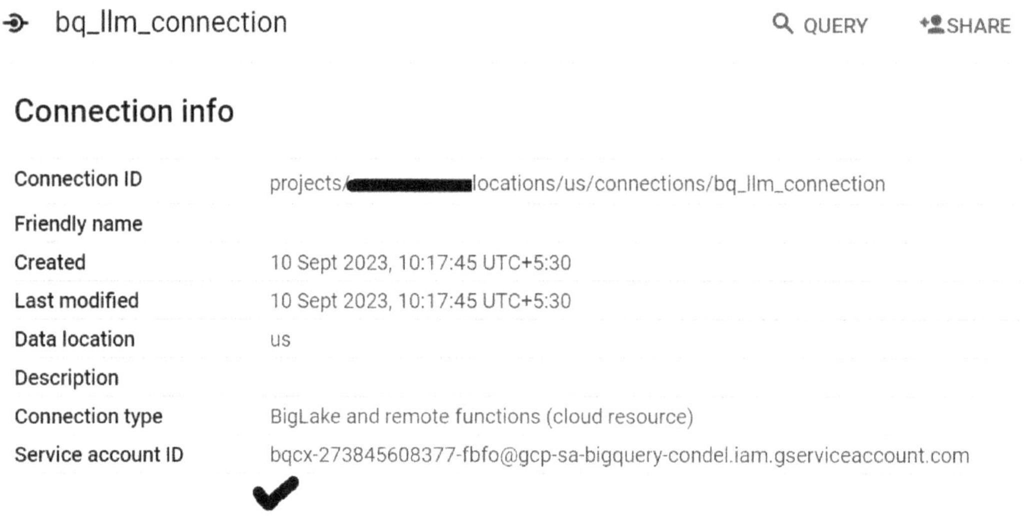

➔ bq_llm_connection   🔍 QUERY   ⁺🧑 SHARE

Connection info

Connection ID	projects/▬▬▬▬▬locations/us/connections/bq_llm_connection
Friendly name	
Created	10 Sept 2023, 10:17:45 UTC+5:30
Last modified	10 Sept 2023, 10:17:45 UTC+5:30
Data location	us
Description	
Connection type	BigLake and remote functions (cloud resource)
Service account ID	bqcx-273845608377-fbfo@gcp-sa-bigquery-condel.iam.gserviceaccount.com

Figure 10.7: The Connection info page

As you can see, a service account ID has been created for your connection. Make a note of that.

Step 4 – grant permissions to the service account to access the Vertex AI service

For BigQuery to access the Vertex AI service as a remote function, we need to provide the necessary permissions to the external connection that's been created.

To do that, select **IAM** from Google Cloud Console's hamburger menu (the three lines in the top-left corner), and on the IAM page that opens, on the right, click **GRANT ACCESS** in the **VIEW BY PRINCIPALS** tab. Enter the service account ID you noted in the previous step in the **New principals** section. All these pointers are highlighted in the following figure with a black checkmark:

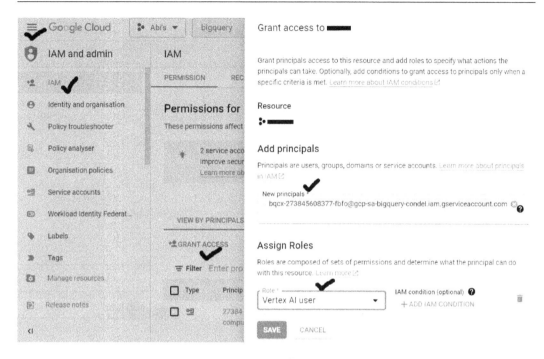

Figure 10.8: IAM configuration page

Enter the necessary details to add the permissions, as shown in the preceding figure, and click **SAVE**.

At this point, we have the data, external connection, and permissions to create the LLM model in BigQuery by accessing the Vertex AI service as a remote function.

Step 5 – create the remote model in BigQuery

Create a remote model in BigQuery and name it `text_descriptor`. This will use the `CLOUD_AI_LARGE_LANGUAGE_MODEL_V1` remote service type (it is the Vertex AI LLM for text generation: `text-bison`) as a hosted remote function in BigQuery.

In the BigQuery query editor, run the following statement:

```
CREATE OR REPLACE MODEL bq_llm.text_descriptor
REMOTE WITH CONNECTION `us.bq_llm_connection`
OPTIONS (remote_service_type = 'CLOUD_AI_LARGE_LANGUAGE_MODEL_V1');
```

Note that the CONNECTION keyword is followed by the connection's name – that is, us.bq_llm_connection. This is because we created the connection in the US region with the name bq_llm_connection. If you have chosen different values for this, use your connection attributes correctly. Click **RUN**; this will create the model, as shown here:

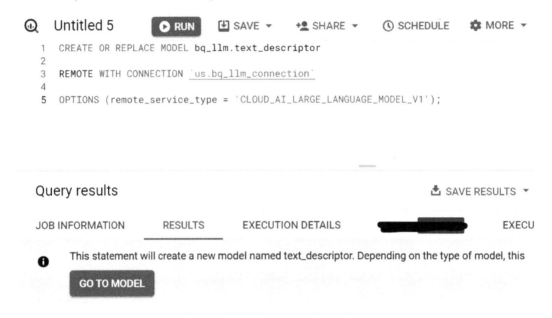

Figure 10.9: BigQuery model creation

As we can see, the model has been created, and you have a **GO TO MODEL** button in the **RESULTS** tab. Upon clicking that, you should be able to see the model's details.

Step 6 – query the dataset

Now that the model has been created, you should be able to use the model and generate text on the dataset we created earlier. But before that, let's view the dataset on which we are creating the Generative AI application. We created the words table and inserted three rows in it. Let's run the query in the BigQuery query editor:

```
select * from bq_llm.words;
```

You should see the results shown in the following screenshot:

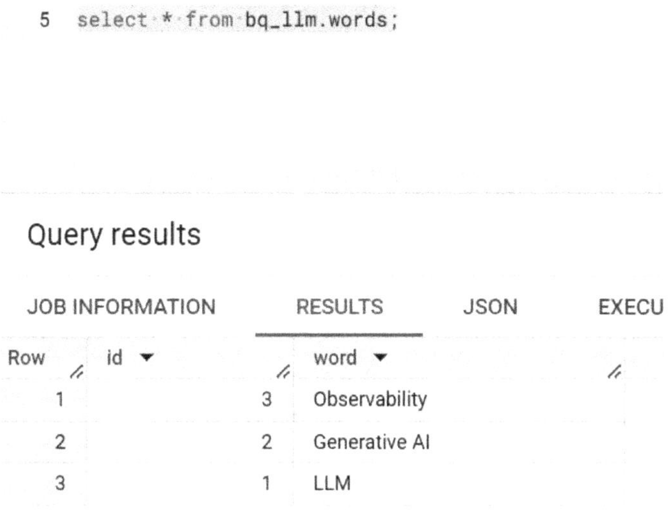

```
5   select * from bq_llm.words;
```

Query results

JOB INFORMATION	RESULTS	JSON	EXECU
Row / id ▼	/ word ▼		/
1	3	Observability	
2	2	Generative AI	
3	1	LLM	

Figure 10.10: Querying the table words to view our data

Step 7 – generate text (create an LLM application) using only SQL

Now that the model has been created and we know the data that we are working with, let's go ahead and use the model to generate text on the data we have stored.

Run the following query in the BigQuery query editor to generate text for the three words we have stored in the words table:

```
SELECT *
FROM
ML.GENERATE_TEXT(
MODEL `bq_llm.text_descriptor`,
(
SELECT
CONCAT('Can you read the word and create a two line description for
it:', word)
AS prompt
from `bq_llm.words`
),
STRUCT(
0.8 AS temperature,
100 AS max_output_tokens,
TRUE AS flatten_json_output));
```

Let's look at the components of the SELECT query:

- ML.GENERATE_TEXT is the construct for accessing the Vertex AI model in BigQuery to perform text generation.

- CONCAT is the construct that appends the prompt and the database value. We are concatenating the prompt, Can you read the word and create a two-line description for it:, and the value in the word field from the words table.

- prompt is the construct that tells the model what to generate. There is a whole subject called *prompt engineering* or *prompt design* that deserves to be discussed in detail, but this is outside the scope of this chapter. You can learn more about it here: https://cloud.google.com/vertex-ai/docs/generative-ai/learn/introduction-prompt-design.

- temperature is the prompt parameter that controls the randomness of the model's response. If you want your model to respond less wildly, choose a smaller value.

- max_output_tokens is the number of words you want from the model in response.

- flatten_json_output is a Boolean that, if set to true, returns a flattened text that is relatively more understandable, and it is extracted from the JSON response.

Once you run the aforementioned query, you should be able to see the results from the model:

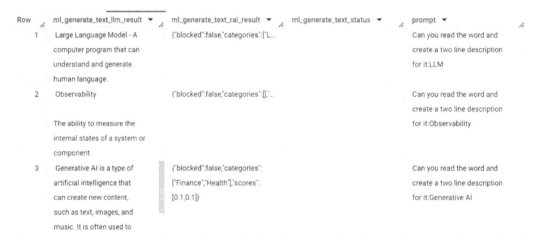

Figure 10.11: Generating text using ML.GENERATE_TEXT

The preceding screenshot shows the query results, including two notable fields, ml_generate_text_llm_result and ml_generate_text_rai_result, in the response. Let's look at these response attributes:

- ml_generate_text_llm_result is the response field that contains the generated text content.

- `ml_generate_text_rai_result` is the response field that contains the safety attributes with a pre-built content filter and adjustable threshold that is enabled in the API to avoid unsafe responses from the API. The text response will be blocked if the response exceeds the safety threshold. This also accounts for how smoothly we have incorporated responsible AI in our solution using the Vertex AI API in BigQuery.

That's it! We have created a simple LLM application in BigQuery using only SQL queries.

This was a simple hands-on exercise that was included to engage your learning about databases, data warehouses, and data modeling in creating an LLM application. Try it out for your own use cases.

Vector databases

As I promised, let me brief you a little about vector databases. I have taken the approach of explaining it to a 10-year-old; you can skip to the last paragraph of this section if you are not comfortable with this explanation.

Imagine that you have a big box of toys. Each toy has many different features, such as its shape, color, size, and material. You could describe each toy in words, but that would be very time-consuming and difficult to search through. A vector database is a way to represent each toy as a set of numbers, called a vector. Each number in the vector represents a different feature of the toy.

For example, the first number might represent the toy's shape, the second number might represent its color, and so on. Vector databases are very efficient for searching. For example, you could search for all the toys that are red and ball-shaped. The vector database would simply compare the vectors of all of the toys to find the ones that match your query.

Vector databases are specialized databases for storing and querying vectors, which are mathematical representations of data. Vector databases store and query vectors, which represent data in a high-dimensional space. This enables Generative AI models to learn complex relationships between data and generate new content. Google Cloud offers vector database options such as Vertex AI Vector Search, Cloud SQL for PostgreSQL vector extension (pgvector), and more. You can also choose to use the Vertex AI Vector Search service to store for and search vectors in BigQuery.

Summary

In this chapter, we walked through the phenomenon that has taken the world by storm – LLMs. We covered some fundamental topics around the evolution, basics, and principles of LLMs, the differences between data model design for good old analytical applications, and looked at LLM applications with some real-world use cases. Then, we discussed some data model considerations, techniques, best practices, and ethical considerations for data modeling design for LLM use cases. We also extended our learning to a simple hands-on LLM application development exercise.

LLMs and Generative AI services such as BigQuery and Vertex AI open up countless opportunities and potential business insights across industries by enabling us to work with diverse data formats and sources. I hope this chapter was able to equip you with a foundational insight into the world of LLMs and their applications while helping you prepare your data and design to handle the scaling use cases, challenges, and responsibilities.

Onward and upward!

I hope you enjoyed learning about cloud database design and modeling, hands-on, through these chapters. Try to apply this learning and awareness to projects at work, learning, or business applications. If you end up getting ground-breaking ideas or solving complex day-to-day data problems with ideas and concepts you've learned, feel free to reach out to me on my socials at `https://abirami.dev`. I would be thrilled to feature your experience in some of our developer community programs. You can learn about this at `https://codevipassana.dev`.

Index

D

Packtpub.com

Subscribe to our online digital library for full access to over 7,000 books and videos, as well as industry leading tools to help you plan your personal development and advance your career. For more information, please visit our website.

Why subscribe?

- Spend less time learning and more time coding with practical eBooks and Videos from over 4,000 industry professionals

- Improve your learning with Skill Plans built especially for you

- Get a free eBook or video every month

- Fully searchable for easy access to vital information

- Copy and paste, print, and bookmark content

Did you know that Packt offers eBook versions of every book published, with PDF and ePub files available? You can upgrade to the eBook version at Packtpub.com and as a print book customer, you are entitled to a discount on the eBook copy. Get in touch with us at customercare@packtpub.com for more details.

At www.packtpub.com, you can also read a collection of free technical articles, sign up for a range of free newsletters, and receive exclusive discounts and offers on Packt books and eBooks.

Other Books You May Enjoy

If you enjoyed this book, you may be interested in these other books by Packt:

Data Engineering with Google Cloud Platform

Adi Wijaya

ISBN: 9781800561328

- Load data into BigQuery and materialize its output for downstream consumption
- Build data pipeline orchestration using Cloud Composer
- Develop Airflow jobs to orchestrate and automate a data warehouse
- Build a Hadoop data lake, create ephemeral clusters, and run jobs on the Dataproc cluster
- Leverage Pub/Sub for messaging and ingestion for event-driven systems
- Use Dataflow to perform ETL on streaming data
- Unlock the power of your data with Data Studio
- Calculate the GCP cost estimation for your end-to-end data solutions

Machine Learning with BigQuery ML

Alessandro Marrandino

ISBN: 9781800560307

- Discover how to prepare datasets to build an effective ML model
- Forecast business KPIs by leveraging various ML models and BigQuery ML
- Build and train a recommendation engine to suggest the best products for your customers using BigQuery ML
- Develop, train, and share a BigQuery ML model from previous parts with AI Platform Notebooks
- Find out how to invoke a trained TensorFlow model directly from BigQuery
- Get to grips with BigQuery ML best practices to maximize your ML performance

Packt is searching for authors like you

If you're interested in becoming an author for Packt, please visit `authors.packtpub.com` and apply today. We have worked with thousands of developers and tech professionals, just like you, to help them share their insight with the global tech community. You can make a general application, apply for a specific hot topic that we are recruiting an author for, or submit your own idea.

Share Your Thoughts

Now you've finished *Database Design and Modeling with Google Cloud*, we'd love to hear your thoughts! Scan the QR code below to go straight to the Amazon review page for this book and share your feedback or leave a review on the site that you purchased it from.

`https://packt.link/r/1-804-61145-X`

Your review is important to us and the tech community and will help us make sure we're delivering excellent quality content.

Download a free PDF copy of this book

Thanks for purchasing this book!

Do you like to read on the go but are unable to carry your print books everywhere?

Is your eBook purchase not compatible with the device of your choice?

Don't worry, now with every Packt book you get a DRM-free PDF version of that book at no cost.

Read anywhere, any place, on any device. Search, copy, and paste code from your favorite technical books directly into your application.

The perks don't stop there, you can get exclusive access to discounts, newsletters, and great free content in your inbox daily

Follow these simple steps to get the benefits:

1. Scan the QR code or visit the link below

https://packt.link/free-ebook/9781804611456

2. Submit your proof of purchase
3. That's it! We'll send your free PDF and other benefits to your email directly

www.ingramcontent.com/pod-product-compliance
Lightning Source LLC
Chambersburg PA
CBHW080522060326
40690CB00022B/5003